Hardy Ornamental Flowering Trees and Shrubs

A. D. Webster

Contents

PREFACE TO FIRST EDITION, 1893. 7
PREFACE TO SECOND AND CHEAP EDITION, 1897. 9
HARDY ORNAMENTAL FLOWERING TREES & SHRUBS. 10
ADDENDA. 200
INDEX. 219

HARDY ORNAMENTAL FLOWERING TREES AND SHRUBS

BY

A. D. Webster

PREFACE TO FIRST EDITION, 1893.

This book has been written and is published with the distinct object in view of bringing home to the minds of planters of Hardy Trees and Shrubs, the fact that the monotonous repetition, in at least nine-tenths of our Parks and Gardens, of such Trees as the Elm, the Lime, and the Oak, and such Shrubs as the Cherry Laurel and the Privet, is neither necessary nor desirable. There is quite a host of choice and beautiful flowering species, which, though at present not generally known are yet perfectly hardy, of the simplest culture, and equally well adapted for the ornamentation of our Public and Private Parks and Gardens.

Of late years, with the marked decline in the cultivation of Coniferous Trees, many of which are ill adapted for the climate of this country, the interest in our lovely flowering Trees and Shrubs has been greatly revived. This fact has been well exemplified in the numerous enquiries after these subjects, and the space devoted to their description and modes of cultivation in the Horticultural Press.

In the hope, too, of helping to establish a much-desired standard of nomenclature, I have followed the generic names adopted by the authors of *The Genera Plantarum*, and the specific names and orthography, as far as I have been able, of the *Index Kewensis*; and where possible I have given the synonyms, the date of introduction, and the native country. The alphabetical arrangement that has been adopted, both with regard to the genera and species, it is hoped, will greatly facilitate the work of reference to its pages. The descriptive notes and hints on cultivation, the selected lists of Trees and Shrubs for various special purposes, and the calendarial list which indicates the flowering season of the different species, may be considered all the more valuable for being concisely written, and made readily accessible by means of the Index.

No work written on a similar plan and treating solely of Hardy Ornamental Flowering Trees and Shrubs has hitherto been published; and it is not supposed for a moment that the present one will entirely supply the deficiency; but should it meet with any measure of public approval, it may be the means of paving the way towards the publication of a more elaborate work--and one altogether more worthy of the interesting and beautiful Flowering Trees and Shrubs that have been found suitable for planting in the climate of the British Isles.

Of the fully thirteen hundred species and varieties of Trees and Shrubs enumerated, all may be depended upon as being hardy in some part of the country. Several of them, and particularly those introduced from China and Japan, have not before been included in a book of this character. Trials for the special purpose of testing the hardiness of the more tender kinds have been instituted and carried out in several favoured parts of England and Ireland.

A.D.W.
HOLLYDALE, WOBURN.

PREFACE TO SECOND AND CHEAP EDITION, 1897.

The First Edition of Hardy Ornamental Flowering Trees and Shrubs having been sold out, it has been considered desirable to run off a second and cheap edition on exactly similar lines to the first, and previous to the more elaborate illustrated edition which is now in hand.

A.D.W.
BOXMOOR, HERTS, 1897.

HARDY ORNAMENTAL FLOWERING TREES & SHRUBS.

ABELIA.

ABELIA CHINENSIS (syn A. rupestris).--The Rock Abelia China, 1844. This is a neat, twiggy shrub, growing from 2 ft. to 3 ft. high, with slender shoots, and very pleasing, shining green serrated leaves. The tubular, sweet-scented flowers are produced in clusters at the ends of the shoots, even the smallest, and are of a very delicate shade of pink--indeed, almost white. It makes an excellent wall plant, but by no means refuses to grow and flower freely without either shelter or protection, provided a fairly rich and well drained soil is provided. From August to October is the flowering period of this handsome deciduous shrub. This is the only really hardy species of the genus, for though the rosy-purple flowered A. floribunda from Mexico has stood for several years uninjured in the South of England, it is not to be relied upon. Both species are readily propagated from cuttings.

A. TRIFLORA.--Himalayan regions, 1847. A half-hardy and beautiful species with small lanceolate, entire leaves, and pretty star-shaped flowers that are white and flushed with pink. The long, narrow, and hairy calyx-lobes give a light and feathery appearance to the flowers, which are produced continuously from May to November. It does best as a wall plant, and several beautiful examples may be seen in and around London, as also at Exeter, and in the South of Ireland.

ADENOCARPUS.

ADENOCARPUS DECORTICANS (syn A. Boissieri).--Spain, 1883. This little known hardy shrub, a native of the Sierra Nevada mountains, in Spain, is one of great beauty, and well worthy of extended culture. The flowers are produced abundantly, and are of a bright yellow colour, resembling those of our common Broom, to which family it is nearly allied. Peaty soil suits it well, and repeated trials have clearly proved that it is hardy, at least in the South of England.

AESCULUS.

AESCULUS CALIFORNICA (syn Pavia californica).--California. This is one of the handsomest species, of low, spreading habit, and blooming freely about midsummer.

AE. GLABRA (syn Ae. rubicunda).--Red-flowered Horse Chestnut. North America, 1820. If only for its neat and moderate growth, and attractive spikes of brightly-coloured flowers, this species must be considered as one of the handsomest and most valuable of small growing trees. Being of moderate size, for we rarely meet with specimens of greater height than 30 feet, and of very compact habit, it is rendered peculiarly suitable for planting in confined spots, and where larger growing and more straggling subjects would be out of place. It withstands soot and smoke well, and is therefore much valued for suburban planting. The long spikes of pretty red flowers are usually produced in great abundance, and as they stand well above the foliage, and are of firm lasting substance, they have a most pleasing and attractive appearance. As there are numerous forms of the red-flowered Horse Chestnut, differing much in the depth of flower colouring, it may be well to warn planters, for some of these have but a faint tinge of pink overlying a dirty yellowish-green groundwork, while the finest and most desirable tree has the flowers of a decided pinky-red. There is a double-flowered variety Ae. glabra flore-pleno (syn Ae. rubicunda flore-pleno) and one of particular merit named Ae. rubicunda Briotii.

AE. HIPPOCASTANUM.--The Common Horse Chestnut. Asia, 1629. A fine hardy free-flowering tree, supposed to have been introduced from Asia, and of which there are several varieties, including a double-flowered, a variegated, and several lobed and cut-leaved forms. The tree needs no description, the spikes of pinky-white flowers, which are produced in great abundance, and ample foliage rendering it one of, if not the handsomest tree of our acquaintance. It gives a pleasing shade, and forms an imposing and picturesque object in the landscape, especially where the conditions of soil--a rich free loam--are provided. Ae. Hippocastanum alba flore-pleno (the double white Horse Chestnut), has a decidedly pyramidal habit of growth, and the flowers, which are larger than those of the species, are perfectly double. It is a very distinct and desirable large growing tree. Ae. Hippocastanum laciniata and Ae. Hippocastanum digitalis are valuable for their divided leaves; while Ae. Hippocastanum foliis variegatis has the foliage rather irregularly variegated.

AE. PARVIFLORA (syn Pavia macrostachya).--Buckeye. North America, 1820. This is very distinct, and possesses feature which are shared by no other hardy tree or shrub in cultivation. Rarely exceeding 12 feet in height, and with a spread of often as much as 20 feet, this shrub forms a perfect hemisphere of foliage, and which, when tipped with the pretty fragrant flowers, renders it one of the most effective and handsome. The foliage is large, and resembles that of the common Horse Chestnut, while the pure white flowers, with their long projecting stamens and red-tipped anthers, are very pretty and imposing when at their best in July. It succeeds well in rich, dampish loam, and as a shrub for standing alone in any conspicuous position it has, indeed, few equals.

AE. PAVIA (syn Pavia rubra).--Red Buckeye. North America, 1711. A small growing and slender-branched tree or shrub, which bears an abundance of brownish-scarlet flowers. There are several good varieties, two of the best being Ae. Pavia atrosanguinea, and Ae. Pavia Whittleyana, with small, brilliant red flowers.

There are several other species, such as Ae. Pavia humilis (syn Pavia humilis) of trailing habit; Ae. flava (syn Pavia flava) bearing pretty yellow flowers; Ae. Pavia macrocarpa (syn Pavia macrocarpa) an open-headed and graceful tree; Ae. flava discolor (syn Pavia discolor); and Ae. chinensis; but they have not been found very amenable to cultivation, except in very favoured parts of the South of England and Ireland.

AILANTHUS.

AILANTHUS GLANDULOSA.--Tree of Heaven. China, 1751. A handsome, fast-growing tree, with large pinnate leaves that are often fully three feet long, and terminal erect clusters of not very showy greenish-white flowers that exhale a rather disagreeable odour. It is one of the most distinct and imposing of pinnate-leaved trees, and forms a neat specimen for the lawn or park. Light loam or a gravelly subsoil suits it well.

AKEBIA.

AKEBIA QUINATA.--Chinese Akebia. China, 1845. This, with its peculiarly-formed and curiously-coloured flowers, though usually treated as a cool greenhouse plant, is yet sufficiently hardy to grow and flower well in many of the southern and western English counties, where it has stood uninjured for many years. It is a pretty twining evergreen, with the leaves placed on long slender petioles, and palmately divided into usually five leaflets. The sweet-scented flowers, particularly so in the evening, are of a purplish-brown or scarlet-purple, and produced in axillary racemes of from ten to a dozen in each. For covering trellis-work, using as a wall plant, or to clamber over some loose-growing specimen shrub, from which a slight protection will also be afforded, the Akebia is peculiarly suitable, and soon ascends to a height of 10 feet or 12 feet. Any ordinary garden soil suits it, and propagation by cuttings is readily affected.

AMELANCHIER.

AMELANCHIER ALNIFOLIA.--Dwarf June Berry. N.W. America, 1888. This is a shrub of great beauty, growing about 8 feet high, and a native of the mountains from British America to California. This differs from A. canadensis in having much larger and more brilliant-tinted fruit, and in its shorter and more compact flower racemes. The shape of the leaves cannot be depended on as a point of recognition, those before me, collected in the native habitat of the plant, differing to a wide extent in size and shape, some being coarsely serrated while others are almost entire.

A. CANADENSIS.--June Berry. Canada, 1746. Unquestionably this is one of the most beautiful and showy of early flowering trees. During the month of April the profusion of snow-white flowers, with which even young specimens are mantled, render the plant conspicuous for a long way off, while in autumn the golden yellow of the dying-off foliage is quite as remarkable. Being perfectly hardy, of free growth, and with no particular desire for certain classes of soils, the June Berry should be widely planted for ornamental effect. In this country it attains to a height of 40 feet, and bears globose crimson fruit. There are several varieties, including A. canadensis rotundifolia, A.

canadensis oblongifolia, and A. canadensis oligocarpa, the latter being by some botanists ranked as a species.

A. VULGARIS.--Common Amelanchier. South of Europe, 1596. This is the only European species, and grows about 16 feet in height. It has been in cultivation in this country for nearly 300 years. Generally this species flowers earlier than the American ones, has rounder and less deeply serrated leaves, but the flowers are much alike. A. vulgaris cretica, from Crete and Dalmatia, is readily distinguished by the soft white hairs with which the under sides of the leaves are thickly covered. To successfully cultivate the Amelanchiers a good rich soil is a necessity, while shelter from cutting winds must be afforded if the sheets of flowers are to be seen in their best form.

AMORPHA.

AMORPHA CANESCENS.--Lead Plant. Missouri, 1812. This is of much smaller growth than A. fruticosa, with neat pinnate foliage, whitened with hoary down, and bearing panicles of bluish-purple flowers, with conspicuous orange anthers. It is a charming shrub, and all the more valuable as it flowers at the end of summer, when few hardy plants are in bloom. To grow it satisfactorily a dry, sandy soil is a necessity.

A. FRUTICOSA.--False Indigo. Carolina, 1724. This is a fast growing shrub of fully 6 feet high, of loose, upright habit, and with pretty pinnate leaves. The flowers are borne in densely packed spikes, and are of a purplish tint with bright yellow protruding anthers and produced at the end of summer. It prefers a dry, warm soil of a sandy or chalky nature, and may readily be increased from cuttings or suckers, the latter being freely produced. Hard cutting back when full size has been attained would seem to throw fresh vigour into the Amorpha, and the flowering is greatly enhanced by such a mode of treatment. A native of Carolina, and perfectly hardy in most parts of the country. Of this species there are several varieties, amongst others, A. fruticosa nana, a dwarf, twiggy plant; A. fruticosa dealbata, with lighter green foliage than the type; and others differing only in the size and width of the leaves.

ANDROMEDA.

ANDROMEDA POLIFOLIA.--An indigenous shrub of low growth, with lanceolate shining leaves, and pretty globose pinky-white flowers. Of it there are two varieties. A. polifolia major and A. polifolia angustifolia, both well worthy of culture for their neat habit and pretty flowers.

See CASSANDRA, CASSIOPE, LEUCOTHOE, OXYDENDRUM, PIERIS, and ZENOBIA.

ARALIA.

ARALIA MANDSHURICA (syn Dimorphanthus mandschuricus).--Manchuria, 1866. There is not much beauty about this Chinese tree, for it is but a big spiny stake, with no branches, and a tuft of palm-like foliage at the top. The flowers, however, are both large and conspicuous, and impart to the tree an interesting and novel appearance. They are individually small, of a creamy-white colour, and produced in long, umbellate racemes, and which when fully developed, from their weight and terminal position, are tilted gracefully to one side. Usually the stem is spiny, with Horse Chestnut-like bark, while the terminal bud, from its large size, as if all the energy of the plant was concentrated in the tip, imparts a curious and somewhat ungainly appearance to the tree. From its curious tropical appearance this species is well worthy of a place in the shrubbery. It is unmindful of soil, if that is of at all fair quality, and may be said to be perfectly hardy over the greater part of the country.

A. SPINOSA.--Angelica Tree. Virginia, 1688. Amongst autumn-flowering shrubs this takes a high place, for in mild seasons it blooms well into October. It grows about 12 feet high, with large tri-pinnate leaves, composed of numerous serrulate leaflets. The individual flowers are small and whitish, but being borne in large branched panicles have a very imposing appearance. It is of free growth, and produces suckers abundantly.

See also FATSIA.

ARBUTUS.

ARBUTUS ANDRACHNE.--Levant, 1724. This Mediterranean species is of stout growth, with narrow Laurel-like leaves, reddish deciduous bark, and greenish-white flowers that are produced freely in May. A hybrid form, said to have originated between this species and A. Unedo, partakes in part of the nature of both shrubs, but the flowers are larger than those of A. Unedo.

A. MENZIESII (syn A. procera).--Tall Strawberry Tree. North-west America, 1827. This is hardy in many parts of these islands, particularly maritime districts, and is worthy of culture if only for the large racemose panicles of deliciously-scented white flowers, and peculiar metallic-green leaves. The fruit is orange-red, and only about half the size of those of our commonly cultivated species.

A. UNEDO.--Strawberry Tree. Ireland. This is a beautiful evergreen shrub or small-growing tree, sometimes fully 20 feet high, with ovate-lanceolate leaves, and clusters of pure white or yellowish-tinged flowers appearing in September and October. The bright scarlet fruit, about the size of and resembling a Strawberry, is highly ornamental, and when borne in quantity imparts to the plant an unusual and very attractive appearance. Generally speaking, the Arbutus is hardy, although in inland situations it is sometimes killed to the ground in severe winters, but, springing freely from the root, the plant soon becomes re-established. In a young state it suffers too, but after becoming established and a few feet high, the chances of injury are greatly minimised. Three well-marked varieties are A. Unedo coccinea and A. Unedo rubra, bearing scarlet and deep-red flowers, and A. Unedo microphylla, with much smaller leaves than those of the parent plant.

A. UNEDO CROOMEI differs considerably from the former, in having larger foliage, larger clusters of reddish-pink flowers, and the bark of the young shoots of an enticing ruddy, or rather brownish-red colour. It is a very desirable and highly ornamental plant, and one that is well worthy of extended culture.

There are several others, to wit A. photiniaefolia, A. Rollissoni, A. Millerii, with large leaves, and pretty pink flowers, and A. serratifolia, having deeply serrated leaves. Deep, light loam, if on chalk all the better, and a fairly warm and sheltered situation, would seem to suit the Arbutus best.

ARCTOSTAPHYLOS.

ARCTOSTAPHYLOS UVA-URSI.--Bearberry. Britain. A neat shrub of trailing
habit, and with flowers resembling those of the Arbutus, but much smaller. The leaves are entire, dark green in colour, and about an

inch long, and obovate or oblong in shape. Fruit globular, of a bright red, smooth and shining. This is a native shrub, being found in Scotland, northern England and Ireland.

A. ALPINA.--Black Bearberry. Scotland. This is confined to the northern Highlands of Scotland, is of smaller growth, with toothed deciduous leaves, and small drooping flowers of two or three together.

ARISTOLOCHIA.

ARISTOLOCHIA SIPHO.--Dutchman's Pipe. North America, 1763. A large-growing, deciduous climbing shrub, remarkable for its ample foliage, and curiously formed yellow and purple streaked flowers. A native of North America, it is perfectly hardy in this country, and makes an excellent wall plant where plenty of space can be afforded for the rambling branches. What a pity it is that so ornamental a climber, whose big, dark-green leaves overlap each other as if intended for keeping a house cool in warm weather, is not more generally planted. It does well and grows fast in almost any soil.

ASIMINA.

ASIMINA TRILOBA.--Virginian Papaw. Pennsylvania, 1736. This is a curious and uncommon shrub that one rarely sees outside the walls of a botanic garden. The flowers are dark purple or chocolate brown, fully 2 inches across, and succeeded by a yellow, oblong, pulpy fruit, that is relished by the natives, and from which the name of North American Custard Apple has been derived. In this country it is quite at home, growing around London to quite 12 feet in height, but it wants a warm, dry soil, and sunny sheltered situation. As a wall plant it does well.

AZARA.

AZARA MICROPHYLLA.--Chili, 1873. This is the only recognised hardy species, and probably the best from an ornamental point of view. In mild seaside districts it may succeed as a standard in the open ground, but generally it is cultivated as a wall plant, and for which it is peculiarly suitable. The small dark green, glossy leaves are thickly arranged on the nearly horizontal branches, while the flowers, if they lack in point of showiness, are deliciously fragrant and plentifully produced. For wall-covering, especially in an eastern aspect, it is one of the neatest of shrubs.

Other species in cultivation are A. serrata, A. lanceolata, and A. integrifolia, but for general planting, and unless under the most favoured conditions, they are not to be recommended. The Azaras are by no means particular about the quality of soil in which they are planted, and succeed well even in stiffish loam, bordering on clay.

BACCHARIS.

BACCHARIS HALIMIFOLIA.--Groundsel Tree or Sea Purslane. North America.
For seaside planting this is an invaluable shrub, as it succeeds well down even to high water mark, and where it is almost lashed by the salt spray. The flowers are not very ornamental, resembling somewhat those of the Groundsel, but white with a tint of purple. Leaves obovate in shape, notched, and thickly covered with a whitish powder, which imparts to them a pleasing glaucous hue. Any light soil that is tolerably dry suits well the wants of this shrub, but it is always seen in best condition by the seaside. Under favourable conditions it attains to a height of 12 feet, with a branch spread nearly as much in diameter. A native of the North American coast from Maryland to

Florida.

B. PATAGONICA.--Megallan. This is a very distinct and quite hardy species, with small deep green leaves and white flowers. It succeeds under the same conditions as the latter.

BERBERIDOPSIS.

BERBERIDOPSIS CORALLINA.--Coral Barberry. Chili, 1862. This handsome evergreen, half-climbing shrub is certainly not so well known as its merits entitle it to be. Unfortunately it is not hardy in every part of the country, though in the southern and western English counties, but especially within the influence of the sea, it succeeds well as a wall plant, and charms us with its globular, waxy, crimson or coral-red flowers. The spiny-toothed leaves approach very near those of some of the Barberries, and with which the plant is nearly allied. It seems to do best in a partially shady situation, and in rich light loam.

BERBERIS.

BERBERIS AQUIFOLIUM (syn Mahonia Aquifolium).--Holly-leaved Barberry. North America, 1823. This justly ranks as one of the handsomest, most useful, and easily-cultivated of all hardy shrubs. It will grow almost any where, and in any class of soil, though preferring a fairly rich loam. Growing under favourable conditions to a height of 6 feet, this North American shrub forms a dense mass of almost impenetrable foliage. The leaves are large, dark shining green, thickly beset with spines, while the deliciously-scented yellow flowers, which are produced at each branch tip, render the plant particularly attractive in spring. It is still further valuable both on account of the rich autumnal tint of the foliage, and pretty plum colour of the plentifully produced fruit.

B. AQUIFOLIUM REPENS (syn Mahonia repens).--Creeping Barberry. This is of altogether smaller growth than the preceding, but otherwise they seem nearly allied. From its dense, dwarf growth, rising as it rarely does more than a foot from the ground, and neat foliage, this Barberry is particularly suitable for edging beds, or forming a low evergreen covering for rocky ground or mounds.

B. ARISTATA, a native of Nepaul, is a vigorous-growing species, resembling somewhat our native plant, with deeply serrated leaves, brightly tinted bark, and yellow flowers. It is of erect habit, branchy, and in winter is rendered very conspicuous by reason of the bright reddish colour of the leafless branches.

B. BEALEI (syn Mahonia Bealli).--Japan. This species is one of the first to appear in bloom, often by the end of January the plant being thickly studded with flowers. It is a handsome shrub, of erect habit, the leaves of a yellowish-green tint, and furnished with long, spiny teeth. The clusters of racemes of deliciously fragrant yellow flowers are of particular value, being produced so early in the season.

B. BUXIFOLIA (syn B. dulcis and *B. microphylla*).--Straits of Magellan, 1827. A neat and erect-growing shrub of somewhat stiff and upright habit, and bearing tiny yellow flowers. This is a good rockwork plant, and being of neat habit, with small purplish leaves, is well worthy of cultivation.

B. CONGESTIFLORA, from Chili, is not yet well-known, but promises to become a general favourite with lovers of hardy shrubs. It is of unusual appearance for a Barberry, with long, decumbent branches, which are thickly covered with masses of orange-yellow flowers. The branch-tips, being almost leafless and smothered with flowers, impart to the plant a striking, but distinctly ornamental appearance.

B. DARWINII.--Chili, 1849. This is, perhaps, the best known and most ornamental of the family. It forms a dense bush, sometimes 10 feet high, with dark glossy leaves, and dense racemes of orange-yellow flowers, produced in April and May, and often again in the autumn.

B. EMPETRIFOLIA.--Straits of Magellan, 1827. This is a neat-habited and dwarf evergreen species, that even under the best cultivation rarely exceeds 2 feet in height. It is one of the hardiest species, and bears, though rather sparsely, terminal golden-yellow flowers, which are frequently produced both in spring and autumn. For its compact growth and neat foliage it is alone worthy of culture.

B. FORTUNEI (syn Mahonia Fortunei).--China, 1846. This is rather a rare species in cultivation, with finely toothed leaves, composed of about seven leaflets, and bearing in abundance clustered racemes of individually small yellow flowers. A native of China, and requiring a warm, sunny spot to do it justice.

B. GRACILIS (syn Mahonia gracilis).--Mexico. A pretty, half-hardy species, growing about 6 feet high, with slender branches, and shining-green leaves with bright red stalks. Flowers small, in 3-inch long racemes, deep yellow with bright red pedicels. Fruit globular, deep purple.

B. ILICIFOLIA (syn B. Neumanii).--South America, 1791. This is another handsome evergreen species from South America, and requires protection in this country. The thick, glossy-green leaves, beset with spines, and large orange-red flowers, combine to make this species one of great interest and beauty.

B. JAPONICA (syn Mahonia japonica).--Japan. This is not a very satisfactory shrub in these isles, although in warm seaside districts, and when planted in rich loam, on a gravelly subsoil, it forms a handsome plant with noble foliage, and deliciously fragrant yellow flowers.

B. NEPALENSIS (syn Mahonia nepalensis).--Nepaul Barberry. This is a noble Himalayan species that one rarely sees in good condition in this country, unless when protected by glass. The long, chalky-white stems, often rising to 8 feet in height, are surmounted by dense clusters of lemon-yellow flowers. Planted outdoors, this handsome and partly evergreen Barberry must have the protection of a wall.

B. NERVOSA (syn Mahonia glumacea).--North America, 1804. This, with its terminal clusters of reddish-yellow flowers produced in spring, is a highly attractive North-west American species. It is of neat and compact growth, perfectly hardy, but as yet it is rare in cultivation. The autumnal leafage-tint is very attractive.

B. PINNATA (syn Mahonia facicularis).--A native of Mexico, this species is of stout growth, with long leaves, that are thickly furnished with sharp spines. The yellow flowers are produced abundantly, and being in large bunches render the plant very conspicuous. It is, unfortunately, not very hardy, and requires wall protection to do it justice.

B. SINENSIS.--China, 1815. This is a really handsome and distinct species, with twiggy, deciduous branches, from the undersides of the arching shoots of which the flowers hang in great profusion. They are greenish-yellow inside, but of a dark brownish-crimson without, while the leaves are small and round, and die off crimson in autumn.

B. STENOPHYLLA, a hybrid between B. Darwinii and B. empetrifolia, is one of the handsomest forms in cultivation, the wealth of golden-yellow flowers being remarkable, as is also the dark purple berries. It is very hardy, and of the freest growth.

B. TRIFOLIOLATA (syn Mahonia trifoliolata).--Mexico, 1839. This is a very distinct and beautiful Mexican species that will only succeed around London as a wall plant. It grows about a yard high, with leaves fully 3 inches long, having three terminal sessile leaflets, and slender leaf stalks often 2 inches long. The ternate leaflets are of a glaucous blue colour, marbled with dull green, and very delicately veined. Flowers small, bright yellow, and produced in few-flowered axillary racemes on short peduncles. The berries are small, globular, and light red.

B. TRIFURCA (syn Mahonia trifurca).--China, 1852. This is a shrub of neat low growth, but it does not appear to be at all plentiful.

B. VULGARIS.--Common Barberry. This is a native species, with oblong leaves, and terminal, drooping racemes of yellow flowers. It is chiefly valued for the great wealth of orange-scarlet fruit. There are two very distinct forms, one bearing silvery and the other black fruit, and named respectively B. vulgaris fructo-albo and B. vulgaris fructo-nigro.

B. WALLICHIANA (syn B. Hookeri).--Nepaul, 1820. This is exceedingly ornamental, whether as regards the foliage, flowers, or fruit. It is of dense, bushy growth, with large, dark green spiny leaves, and an abundance of clusters of clear yellow flowers. The berries are deep violet-purple, and fully half-an-inch long. Being perfectly hardy and of free growth it is well suited for extensive planting.

BERCHEMIA.

BERCHEMIA VOLUBILIS.--Climbing Berchemia. Carolina, 1714. A rarely seen, deciduous climber, bearing rather inconspicuous greenish-yellow flowers, succeeded by attractive, violet-tinted berries. The foliage is neat and pretty, the individual leaves being ovate in shape and slightly undulated or wavy. It is a twining shrub that in this country, even under favourable circumstances, one rarely sees ascending to a greater height than about 12 feet. Sandy peat and a shady site suits it best, and so placed it will soon cover a low-growing tree or bush much in the way that our common Honeysuckle does. It is propagated from layers or cuttings.

BIGNONIA.

BIGNONIA CAPREOLATA--Virginia and other parts of America, 1710. This is not so hardy as to be depended upon throughout the country generally, though in the milder parts of England and Ireland it succeeds well as a wall plant. It is a handsome climbing shrub, with long, heart-shaped leaves, usually terminating in branched tendrils, and large orange flowers produced singly.

BILLARDIERA.

BILLARDIERA LONGIFLORA.--Blue Apple Berry. Van Diemen's Land, 1810. If
only for its rich, blue berries, as large as those of a cherry, this otherwise elegant climbing shrub is well worthy of a far greater share of attention than it has yet received, for it must be admitted that it is far from common. The greenish bell-shaped blossoms produced in May are, perhaps, not very attractive, but this is more than compensated

for by the highly ornamental fruit, which renders the plant an object of great beauty about mid-September. Leaves small and narrow, on slender, twining stems, that clothe well the lower half of a garden wall in some sunny favoured spot. Cuttings root freely if inserted in sharp sand and placed in slight heat, while seeds germinate quickly.

BRYANTHUS.

BRYANTHUS ERECTUS.--Siberia. This is a pretty little Ericaceous plant, nearly allied to Menziesia, and with a plentiful supply of dark-green leaves. The flowers, which are borne in crowded clusters at the points of the shoots, are bell-shaped, and of a pleasing reddish-lilac colour. It wants a cool, moist peaty soil, and is perfectly hardy. When in a flowering stage the Bryanthus is one of the brightest occupants of the peat bed, and is a very suitable companion for such dwarf plants as the Heaths, Menziesias, and smaller growing Kalmias.

B. EMPETRIFORMIS (syn Menziesia empetrifolia).--North America, 1829. This is a compact, neat species, and well suited for alpine gardening. The flowers are rosy-purple, and produced abundantly.

BUDDLEIA.

BUDDLEIA GLOBOSA.--Orange Ball Tree. Chili, 1774. A shrubby species, ranging in height from 12 feet to 20 feet, and the only one at all common in gardens. Favoured spots in Southern England would seem to suit the plant fairly well, but to see it at its best one must visit some of the maritime gardens of North Wales, where it grows stout and strong, and flowers with amazing luxuriance. Where it thrives it must be ranked amongst the most beautiful of wall plants, for few, indeed, are the standard specimens that are to be met with, the protection afforded by a wall being almost a necessity in its cultivation. The leaves are linear-lanceolate, and covered with a dense silvery tomentum on the under side, somewhat rugose above, and partially deciduous. Flowers in small globular heads, bright orange or yellow, and being plentifully produced are very showy in early summer. It succeeds well in rich moist loam on gravel.

B. LINDLEYANA.--China, 1844. This has purplish-red flowers and angular twigs, but it cannot be relied upon unless in very sheltered and mild parts of the country.

B. PANICULATA (syn B. crispa).--Nepaul, 1823. This may at once be distinguished by its curly, woolly leaves, and fragrant lilac flowers. It is a desirable species, but suffers from our climate.

BUPLEURUM.

BUPLEURUM FRUTICOSUM.--Hare's Ear. South Europe, 1596. A small-growing,
branching shrub, with obovate-lanceolate leaves, and compound umbels of yellowish flowers. It is more curious than beautiful.

CAESALPINIA.

CAESALPINIA SEPIARIA (syn C. japonica).--India, 1857. This is as yet a comparatively little known shrub, but one that from its beauty and hardihood is sure to become a general favourite. Planted out in a light, sandy, peaty soil, and where fully exposed, this shrub has done well, and proved itself a suitable subject for the climate of England at least. The hard prickles with which both stem and branches are provided renders the shrub of rather formidable appearance, while the leaves are of a peculiarly pleasing soft-green tint. For the flowers, too, it is well worthy of attention, the pinky anthers contrasting so markedly with the deep yellow of the other portions of the flower. They are arranged in long racemes, and show well above the foliage.

CALLUNA.

CALLUNA VULGARIS (syn Erica vulgaris).--Common Ling on Heather. This is the commonest native species, with purplish-pink flowers on small pedicels. There are many very distinct and beautiful-flowering forms, the following being some of the best: C. vulgaris alba, white-flowered; C. vulgaris Hammondi, C. vulgaris minor, and C. vulgaris pilosa, all white-flowered forms; C. vulgaris Alportii, and C. vulgaris Alportii variegata, the former bearing rich crimson flowers, and the latter with distinctly variegated foliage; C. vulgaris argentea, and C. vulgaris aurea, with silvery-variegated and golden foliage; C. vulgaris flore-pleno, a most beautiful and free-growing variety, with double flowers; C. vulgaris Foxii, a dwarf plant that does not flower freely; and C. vulgaris pumila, and C. vulgaris dumosa, which are of small cushion-like growth.

CALOPHACA.

CALOPHACA WOLGARICA.--Siberia, 1786. This member of the Pea family is
of dwarf, branching growth, thickly clothed with glandular hairs, and bears yellow flowers, succeeded by reddish-purple pods. It is of no special importance as an ornamental shrub, and is most frequently seen grafted on the Laburnum, though its natural easy habit of growth is far preferable. Hailing from Siberia, it may be considered as fairly hardy at least.

CALYCANTHUS.

CALYCANTHUS FLORIDUS.--Carolina Allspice. Carolina, 1726. If only for the purplish-red, pleasantly-scented flowers, this North American shrub is worthy of extensive culture. The hardiness, accommodating nature, and delicious perfume of its brightly-coloured flowers render this shrub one of the choicest subjects for the shrubbery or edges of the woodland path. It is of easy though compact growth, reaching in favourable situations a height of 12 feet, and with ovate leaves that are slightly pubescent. Growing best in good fairly moist loam, where partial shade is afforded, the sides of woodland drives and paths will suit this Allspice well; but it wants plenty of room for branch-development. There are several nursery forms of this shrub, such as C. floridus glaucus, C. floridus asplenifolia, and C. floridus nanus, all probably distinct enough, but of no superior ornamental value to the parent plant.

C. OCCIDENTALIS.--Californian or Western Allspice. California, 1831. This is larger in all its parts than the former, and for decorative purposes is even preferable to that species. The flowers are dark crimson, and nearly twice as large as those of C. floridus, but rather more sparsely produced. This is a very distinct and desirable species, and one that can be recommended for lawn and park planting, but, like the former, it delights to grow in a rather moist and shady situation.

CARAGANA.

CARAGANA ARBORESCENS.--Siberian Pea Tree. Siberia, 1752. On account of its great hardihood, this is a very desirable garden shrub or small-growing tree. The bright-yellow, pea-shaped flowers are very attractive, while the deep-green, pinnate foliage imparts to the tree a somewhat unusual but taking appearance. Soil would not seem to be of much moment in the cultivation of this, as, indeed, the other species of Caragana, for it thrives well either on dry, sunny banks, where the soil is light and thin, or in good stiff, yellow loam.

C. FRUTESCENS.--Siberia, 1852. Flowers in May, and is of partially upright habit; while C. Chamlagii, from China, has greenish-yellow flowers, faintly tinted with pinky-purple.

C. MICROPHYLLA (syn C. Altagana), also from Siberia, is smaller of growth than the foregoing, but the flowers are individually larger. It is readily distinguished by the more numerous and hairy leaflets and thorny nature.

C. SPINOSA.--Siberia, 1775. This, as the name indicates, is of spiny growth, and is a beautiful and distinct member of the family. They are all hardy, and readily propagated from seed.

CARDIANDRA.

CARDIANDRA ALTERNIFOLIA.--Japan, 1866. With its neat habit, and pretty
purple-and-white, plentifully-produced flowers, this is worthy of the small amount of care and coddling required to insure its growth in this country. Hailing from Japan, it cannot be reckoned as very hardy, but treated as a wall plant this pretty evergreen does well and flowers freely. It can, however, be said that it is equally hardy with some of the finer kinds of Hydrangea, to which genus it is nearly allied.

CARPENTERIA.

CARPENTERIA CALIFORNICA.--Sierra Nevada, California, 1880. This is undoubtedly one of the most distinct and beautiful of hardy shrubs. That it is perfectly hardy in England and Ireland recently-conducted experiments conclusively prove, as plants have stood unprotected through the past unusually severe winters with which this country has been visited. When in full bloom the pure-white flowers, resembling those of the Japanese Anemone, render it of great beauty, while the light gray leaves are of themselves sufficient to make the shrub one of particular attraction. The Carpenteria is nearly related to the Mock Orange (Philadelphus), grows about 10 feet in height, with lithe and slender branches, and light gray leaves. The flowers, which are pure white with a bunch of yellow stamens, and sweet-scented, are produced usually in fives at the branch-tips, and contrast markedly with the long and light green foliage. It grows and flowers with freedom almost anywhere, but is all the better for wall protection. From cuttings or suckers it is readily increased.

CARYOPTERIS.

CARYOPTERIS MASTACANTHUS.--China and Japan, 1844. This is a neat-growing
Chinese shrub, and of value for its pretty flowers that are produced late in the autumn. It must be ranked as fairly hardy, having stood through the winters of Southern England unprotected; but it is just as well to give so choice a shrub the slight protection afforded by a wall. The leaves are neat, thickly-arranged, and hoary, while the whole plant is twiggy and of strict though by no means formal growth. Flowers lavender-blue, borne at the tips of the shoots, and appearing in succession for a considerable length of time. Light, sandy peat would seem to suit it well, at least in such it grows and flowers freely.

CASSANDRA.

CASSANDRA CALYCULATA (syn Andromeda calyculata).--North America, 1748. This is a handsome species from the Virginian swamps, but one that is rarely seen in a very satisfactory condition in this country. It grows about 18 inches high, with lanceolate dull-green leaves, and pretty pinky-white flowers, individually large and produced abundantly. For the banks of a pond or lake it is a capital shrub and very effective, particularly if massed in groups of from a dozen to twenty plants in each. There are several nursery forms, of which A. calyculata minor is the best and most distinct.

CASSINIA.

CASSINIA FULVIDA (syn Diplopappus chrysophyllus).--New Zealand. This is a neat-growing and beautiful shrub, the rich yellow stems and under sides of the leaves imparting quite a tint of gold to the whole plant. The flowers are individually small, but the whole head, which is creamy-white, is very effective, and contrasts strangely with the golden sheen of this beautiful shrub. It is inclined to be of rather upright growth, is stout and bushy, and is readily increased from cuttings planted in sandy soil in the open border. Probably in the colder parts of the country this charming shrub might not prove perfectly hardy, but all over England and Ireland it seems to be quite at home. The flowers are produced for several months of the year, but are at their best about mid-November, thus rendering the shrub of still further value. It grows freely in sandy peaty soil of a light nature.

CASSIOPE.

CASSIOPE FASTIGIATA (syn Andromeda fastigiata) and **C. TETRAGONA** (syn Andromeda tetragona) are small-growing species, only suitable for rock gardening--the former of neat upright habit, with large pinky-white bells all along the stems; and the latter of bushy growth, with square stems and small white flowers.

CASTANEA.

CASTANEA SATIVA (syn C. vesca and *C. vulgaris*).--Sweet Spanish Chestnut. Asia Minor. Few persons who have seen this tree as an isolated specimen and when in full flower would feel inclined to exclude it from our list. The long, cylindrical catkins, of a yellowish-green colour, are usually borne in such abundance that the tree is, during the month of June, one of particular interest and beauty. So common a tree needs no description, but it may be well to mention that there are several worthy varieties, and which flower almost equally well with the parent tree.

CATALPA.

CATALPA BIGNONIOIDES.--Indian Bean. North America, 1798. When in full bloom this is a remarkable and highly ornamental tree, the curiously-marked flowers and unusually large, bronzy-tinted foliage being distinct from those of almost any other in cultivation. That it is not, perhaps, perfectly hardy in every part of the country is to be regretted, but the numerous fine old specimens that are to be met with all over the country point out that there need be little to fear when assigning this pretty and uncommon tree a position in our parks and gardens. The flowers, produced in spikes at the branch-tips, are white, tinged with violet and speckled with purple and yellow in the throat. Individually the flowers are of large size and very ornamental, and, being produced freely, give the tree a bright and pleasing appearance when at their best. Usually the tree attains to a height of 30 feet in this country, with rather crooked and ungainly branches, and large heart-shaped leaves that are downy beneath. It flourishes well on any free soil, and is an excellent smoke-resisting tree. C. bignonioides aurea is a decided variety, that differs mainly in the leaves being of a desirable golden tint.

C. BUNGEI and C. KAEMPFERI, natives of China and Japan, are hardly to be relied upon, being of tender growth, and, unless in the most favoured situations, suffer from our severe winters. They resemble our commonly cultivated tree.

C. SPECIOSA.--United States, 1879. The Western Catalpa is more erect and taller of growth than C. bignonioides. The flowers too are larger, and of purer white, and with the throat markings of purple and yellow more distinct and not inclined to run into each other. Leaves large, heart-shaped, tapering to a point, of a light pleasing green and soft to the touch. It flowers earlier, and is more hardy than the former.

CEANOTHUS.

CEANOTHUS AMERICANUS.--New Jersey Tea. North America, 1713. A shrub of
4 feet in height, with deep green serrated leaves, that are 2 inches long and pubescent on the under sides. Flowers white, in axillary panicles, and produced in great abundance. This is one of the hardiest species, but succeeds best when afforded wall protection.

C. AZUREUS.--Mexico, 1818. This species, though not hardy enough for every situation, is yet sufficiently so to stand unharmed as a wall plant. It grows from 10 feet to 12 feet high, with deep-green leaves that are hoary on the under sides. The flowers, which are borne in large, axillary panicles, are bright blue, and produced in June and the following months. In a light, dry soil and sunny position this shrub does well as a wall plant, for which purpose it is one of the most ornamental. There are several good nursery forms, of which the following are amongst the best:--C. azureus Albert Pettitt, C. azureus albidus, C. azureus Arnddii, one of the best, C. azureus Gloire de Versailles, and C. azureus Marie Simon.

C. CUNEATUS (syn C. verrucosus).--California, 1848. This is another half-hardy species that requires wall protection, which may also be said of C. Veitchianus, one of the most beautiful of the family, with dense clusters of rich blue flowers and a neat habit of growth.

C. DENTATUS.--California, 1848. With deeply-toothed, shining-green leaves, and deep blue, abundantly-produced flowers, this is a well-known wall plant that succeeds in many parts of the country, particularly within the influence of the sea. It commences flowering in May, and frequently continues until frosts set in. It is a very desirable species, that in favoured situations will grow to fully 10 feet high, and with a spread laterally of nearly the same dimensions.

C. PAPILLOSUS.--California, 1848. This is a straggling bush, with small, blunt leaves, and panicles of pale blue flowers on long footstalks. A native of California and requiring wall protection.

C. RIGIDUS.--Another Californian species, is of upright, stiff growth, a sub-evergreen, with deep purple flowers produced in April and May.

There are other less hardy kinds, including C. floribundus, C.

integerrimus, C. velutinus, and C. divaricatus.

CEDRELA.

CEDRELA SINENSIS (syn Ailanthus flavescens).--China, 1875. This is a fast growing tree, closely resembling the Ailanthus, and evidently quite as hardy. It has a great advantage over that tree, in that the flowers have an agreeable odour, those of the Ailanthus being somewhat sickly and unpleasant. The flowers are individually small, but arranged in immense hanging bunches like those of Koelreuteria paniculata, and being pleasantly scented are rendered still the more valuable. The whole plant has a yellow hue, and the roots have a peculiar reddish colour, and very unlike those of the Ailanthus, which are white.

CELASTRUS.

CELASTRUS SCANDENS.--Climbing Waxwork, or Bitter Sweet. North America,
1736. When planted in rich, moist soil, this soon forms an attractive mass of twisting and twining growths, with distinct glossy foliage in summer and brilliant scarlet fruit in autumn. The flowers are inconspicuous, the chief beauty of the shrub being the show of fruit, which resembles somewhat those of the Spindle Tree (Euonymus), and to which it is nearly allied. A native of North America, it grows from 12 feet to 15 feet high, and is useful in this country for covering arches or tree stems, or for allowing to run about at will on a mound of earth or on rockwork.

CELTIS.

CELTIS AUSTRALIS.--South Europe, 1796. This species is much like C. occidentalis, with black edible fruit. It is not of so tall growth as the American species.

C. OCCIDENTALIS.--Nettle tree. North America, 1656. In general appearance this tree resembles the Elm, to which family it belongs. It has reticulated, cordate-ovate, serrated leaves, with small greenish flowers on slender stalks, and succeeded by blackish-purple fruit about the size of a pea. A not very ornamental tree, at least so far as flowers are concerned, but valuable for lawn planting. It varies very much in the size and shape of the leaves.

CERCIS.

CERCIS CANADENSIS.--North America, 1730. This species resembles C. Siliquastrum, but is of much smaller growth, and bears paler flowers; while C. CHINENSIS, which is not hardy, has large, rosy-pink flowers.

C. SILIQUASTRUM.--Judas Tree. South Europe, 1596. A small-growing tree of some 15 feet in height, and with usually a rather ungainly and crooked mode of growth. It is, however, one of our choicest subjects for ornamental planting, the handsome reniform leaves and rosy-purple flowers produced along the branches and before the leaves appear rendering it a great favourite with planters. There are three distinct forms of this shrub--the first, C. Siliquastrum alba, having pure white flowers; C. Siliquastrum carnea, with beautiful deep pink flowers; and C. Siliquastrum variegata, with neatly variegated foliage, though rather inconstant of character. Natives of South Europe, and amongst the oldest trees of our gardens.

They all succeed best when planted in rather damp loam, and do not object to partial shade, the common species growing well even beneath the drip of large standard trees.

CHIMONANTHUS.

CHIMONANTHUS FRAGRANS.--Winter Flower. Japan, 1766. This Japanese shrub
is certainly one of the most remarkable that could be brought under notice, the deliciously fragrant flowers being produced in abundance during the winter months, and while the plant is yet leafless. Being of slender growth, it is best suited for planting against a wall, the protection thus afforded being just what is wanted for the perfect development of the pretty flowers. C. fragrans grandiflora has larger and less fragrant flowers than the species, and is more common in cultivation.

CHIONANTHUS.

CHIONANTHUS RETUSA.--China, 1852. This is not a very hardy species, and, being less ornamental than the American form, is not to be recommended for general planting.

C. VIRGINICA.--Fringe Tree. North America, 1736. A very ornamental, small-growing tree, with large deciduous leaves and pendent clusters of pure white flowers with long fringe-like petals, and from which the popular name has arisen. It is a charming tree, or rather shrub, in this country, for one rarely sees it more than 10 feet high, and one that, to do it justice, must have a cool and rather damp soil and a somewhat shady situation.

CHOISYA.

CHOISYA TERNATA.--Mexican Orange Flower. Mexico, 1825. A beautiful and distinct shrub that succeeds well in the south and west of England. The evergreen leaves are always fresh and beautiful, and of a dark shining green, while the sweetly-fragrant flowers are produced freely on the apices of last year's wood. They have a singular resemblance to those of the orange, and on the Continent are commonly grown as a substitute for that popular flower. The plant succeeds well in any light, rich soil, and soon grows into a goodly-sized shrub of 4 feet or 5 feet in height. As a wall plant it succeeds well, but in warm, maritime situations it may be planted as a standard without fear of harm. Cuttings root freely if placed in slight heat.

CISTUS.

CISTUS CRISPUS.--Portugal, 1656. This is a distinct species, with curled leaves, and large reddish-purple flowers. It is a valuable ornamental shrub, but, like the others, suffers from the effects of frost.

C. LADANIFERUS.--Gum Cistus. Spain, 1629. A pretty but rather tender shrub, growing in favourable situations to about 4 feet in height. It has lanceolate leaves that are glutinous above, and thickly covered with a whitish tomentum on the under sides, and large and showy white flowers with a conspicuous purple blotch at the base of each petal. Unless in southern and western England, but particularly on the sea-coast, this handsome Portuguese shrub is not to be depended on, in so far as hardihood is concerned.

C. LAURIFOLIUS.--Laurel-leaved Cistus. Spain, 1731. This is the hardiest species in cultivation, but, like the latter, is favourable to the milder parts of these islands, and especially maritime districts. Frequently it rises to 7 feet in height, and is then an object of great beauty, the large yellowish-white flowers showing well above the deep green Laurel-like leaves.

C. MONSPELIENSIS (South of Europe, 1656), and its variety C. monspeliensis florentinus, the former with white, and the latter with white and yellow flowers, are fairly hardy in the milder parts of Britain, but cannot be recommended for general planting.

C. PURPUREUS.--Purple-flowered Cistas. In this species, which may rank next to the latter in point of hardihood, the flowers are of a deep reddish-purple, and with a darker blotch at the base of each petal.

C. SALVIFOLIUS is of loose and rather untidy growth, with rugose leaves and white flowers. It is very variable in character, and the form generally cultivated grows about 4 feet high, and has ovate-lanceolate, almost glabrous leaves.

Other species that are occasionally to be found in collections are C. creticus, with yellow and purple flowers; C. hirsutus, white with yellow blotches at the base of the petals; and C. Clusii, with very large pure-white flowers. All the species of Gum Cistus, or Rock Rose as they are very appropriately named, will be found to succeed best when planted in exalted positions, and among light, though rich, strong soil. They are easy of propagation.

CITRUS.

CITRUS TRIFOLIATA.--Japan, 1869. This is a singular low-growing shrub, with ternate leaves, spiny branches, and fragrant white flowers. It is hardy in many English situations, but does not fruit freely, although the orange-blossom-like flowers are produced very abundantly. A pretty little glossy-leaved shrub that is well worthy of attention, particularly where a cosy corner can be put aside for its cultivation.

CLADRASTIS.

CLADRASTIS AMURENSIS.--Amoor Yellow Wood. Amur, 1880. This is a shrub
that is sure to be extensively cultivated when better known, and more readily procured. It has stood uninjured for several years in various parts of England, so that its hardihood may be taken for granted. The pretty olive-green of the bark, and the greyish-green of the leathery leaves, render the shrub one of interest even in a flowerless state. In July and August the dense spikes of white, or rather yellowish-white flowers are produced freely, and that, too, even before the shrub has attained to a height of 2 feet. It is well worthy of extended culture.

C. TINCTORIA (syn C. lutea and *Virgilia lutea*).--Yellow Wood. North America, 1812. This is a handsome deciduous tree that does well in many parts of the country, and is valued for the rich profusion of white flowers produced, and which are well set-off by the finely-cut pinnate leaves. It is a valuable tree for park and lawn planting, requiring a warm, dry soil, and sunny situation--conditions under which the wood becomes well-ripened, and the flowers more freely produced.

CLEMATIS.

CLEMATIS ALPINA (syn Atragene alpina, A. austriaca and *A. siberica*).--Europe and North America. This is a climbing species with bi-ternately divided leaves, and large flowers with four blue sepals and ten to twelve small flattened organs, which are usually termed petals.

C. CIRRHOSA.--Evergreen Virgin's Bower. Spain, 1596. An interesting, early-flowering species. The flowers, which are greenish-white, are produced in bunches and very effective. It is an evergreen species, of comparative hardihood, and flowers well in sheltered situations.

C. FLAMMULA.--Virgin's Bower. France, 1596. This old and well-known plant is quite hardy in this country. The leaves are pinnate, and the flowers white and fragrant. C. Flammula rubro-marginata is a worthy and beautiful-leaved variety.

C. FLORIDA.--Japan, 1776. This is a beautiful species, and an old inhabitant of English gardens. Leaves composed of usually three oval-shaped leaflets, and unusually bright of tint. The flowers are very large, and pure white. It should be planted in a warm sheltered corner against a wall.

C. GRAVEOLENS.--This is a dwarf shrub, with neatly tripinnate leaves, and solitary, strongly-scented yellow flowers of medium size. A native of Chinese Tartary, and quite hardy.

C. LANUGINOSA.--China, 1851. A handsome species, with large purple leaves that are hairy on the under sides. Flowers pale blue or lilac, very large, and composed of six or eight spreading sepals. C. lanuginosa pallida has immense flowers, often fully half a foot in diameter. Flowers in June.

C. MONTANA.--Nepaul, 1831. This is valuable on account of its flowering in May. It is a free-growing species, with trifoliolate leaves on long footstalks, and large white flowers. C. montana grandiflora is a beautiful variety, having large white flowers so abundantly produced as to hide the foliage. It is quite hardy and of rampant growth.

C. PATENS (syns C. caerulea and ***C. azurea grandiflora***).--Japan, 1836. This has large, pale-violet flowers, and is the parent of many single and double flowered forms. The typical form is, however, very deserving of cultivation, on account of the freedom with which it blooms during June and July from the wood of the previous year. It is perfectly hardy even in the far north.

C. VIORNA.--Leather Flower. United States. This is a showy, small-flowered species, the flowers being campanulate, greenish-white within and purplish without. C. Viorna coccinea is not yet well known, but is one of the prettiest of the small-flowered section. The flowers, which are leathery as in the species, are of a beautiful vermilion on the outside and yellow within.

C. VITALBA.--Lady's Bower, or Old Man's Beard. A handsome native climbing
shrub, common in limestone or chalky districts, and unusually abundant in the southern English counties. Clambering over some neglected fence, often to nearly 20 feet in height, this vigorous-growing plant is seen to best advantage, the three or five-lobed leaves and festoons of greenish-white, fragrant flowers, succeeded by the curious and attractive feathery carpels, render the plant one of the most distinct and desirable of our native wildlings flowering in August.

C. VITICELLA.--Spain, 1569. This is a well-known species of not too rampant growth, and a native of Spain and Italy. The flowers vary a good deal in colour, but in the typical plant they are reddish-purple and produced throughout the summer. Crossed with C. lanuginosa, this species has produced many ornamental and beautiful hybrids, one of the finest and most popular being C. Jackmanii.

C. WILLIAMSI (syn C. Fortunei).--Japan, 1863. The fragrant, white flowers of this species are semi-double, and consist of about 100 oblong-lanceolate sepals narrowed to the base. The leathery leaves are trifoliolate with heart-shaped leaflets. It proves quite hardy, and has several varieties.

GARDEN VARIETIES.--As well as the above there are many beautiful garden hybrids, some of which in point of floral colouring far outvie the parent forms. Included in the following list are a few of the most beautiful kinds:--

Alba Victor.
Alexandra.
Beauty of Worcester.
Belle of Woking.
Blue Gem.
Duchess of Edinburgh.
Edith Jackman.
Fairy Queen.
John Gould Veitch.
Lady Bovill.
Lord Beaconsfield.
Lucie Lemoine.
Madame Baron Veillard.
Miss Bateman.
Mrs. A. Jackman.
Othello.
Prince of Wales.
Rubella.
Star of India.
Stella.
Venus Victrix.
William Kennett.

CLERODENDRON.

CLERODENDRON TRICHOTOMUM.--Japan, 1800. This is at once one of the most beautiful and distinct of hardy shrubs. It is of stout, nearly erect growth, 8 feet high, and nearly as much through, with large, dark-green, ovate leaves, and deliciously fragrant white flowers, with a purplish calyx, and which are at their best in September. Thriving well in any light soil, being of vigorous constitution, and extremely handsome of flower, are qualities which combine to render this shrub one of particular importance in our gardens.

C. FOETIDUM, a native of China, is only hardy in southern and seaside situations, where it forms a bush 5 feet high, with heart-shaped leaves, and large clusters of rosy-pink flowers.

CLETHRA.

CLETHRA ACUMINATA.--Pointed-leaved Pepper Tree. Carolina, 1806. This is not so hardy as C. alnifolia, hailing from the Southern States of North America, but with a little protection is able to do battle with our average English winter. It resembles C. alnifolia, except in the leaves, which are sharp pointed, and like that species delights to grow in damp positions. The flowers are white and drooping, and the growth more robust than is that of C. alnifolia generally. For planting by the pond or lake-side, the Pepper Trees are almost invaluable.

C. ALNIFOLIA.--Alder-leaved Pepper Tree. North America, 1831. A rather stiff-growing shrub of about 5 feet in height, with leaves resembling those of our common Alder, and bearing towards the end of July spikes of almost oppressively fragrant dull-white flowers at the tips of the branches. It is a valuable shrub, not only in an ornamental way, but on account of it thriving in damp, swampy ground, where few others could exist, while at the same time it will succeed and flower freely in almost any good garden soil.

COCCULUS.

COCCULUS CAROLINUS.--This is a half hardy, twining shrub, of free growth when planted by a tree stem in a sheltered wood, but with by no means showy flowers; indeed, it may be described in few words as a shrub of no great beauty nor value.

C. LAURIFOLIUS, from the Himalayas and Japan, is even less hardy than the above, although, used as a wall plant, it has survived for many years in the south and west of England. The foliage of this species is neat and ornamental, but liable to injury from cold easterly winds.

COLLETIA.

COLLETIA CRUCIATA (syn C. bictonensis).--Chili, 1824. With flattened woody branches, and sharp-pointed spines which take the place of leaves, this is at once one of the most singular of hardy flowering shrubs. It forms a stout dense bush about 4 feet high, and bears quantities of small white flowers, which render the plant one of great beauty during the summer months.

C. SPINOSA.--Peru, 1823. This species grows fairly well in some parts of England and Ireland, and is a curious shrub with awl-shaped leaves, and, like the other members of the family, an abundant producer of flowers. It thrives best as a wall plant, and when favourably situated a height of 12 feet is sometimes attained.

COLUTEA.

COLUTEA ARBORESCENS.--Bladder Senna. France, 1548. This is a common plant in English gardens, bearing yellow Pea-shaped flowers, that are succeeded by curious reddish bladder-like seed pods. It grows to 10 feet or 12 feet in height, and is usually of lax and slender growth, but perfectly hardy.

C. CRUENTA (syn C. orientalis and *C. sanguine*).--Oriental Bladder Senna. Levant, 1710. This is a free-growing, round-headed, deciduous bush, of from 6 feet to 8 feet high when fully grown. The leaves are pinnate and glaucous, smooth, and bright green above, and downy beneath. Flowers individually large, of a reddish-copper colour, with a yellow spot at the base of the upper petal. The fruit is an inflated boat-shaped reddish pod. The Bladder Sennas are of very free growth, even in poor, sandy soil, and being highly ornamental, whether in flower or fruit, are to be recommended for extensive cultivation.

CORIARIA.

CORIARIA MYRTIFOLIA.--South Europe, 1629. A deciduous shrub growing to
about 4 feet in height, with Myrtle-like leaves, and upright terminal racemes of not very showy flowers, produced about mid-summer--generally from May to August. For its pretty foliage and the frond-like arrangement of its branches it is principally worthy of culture. From southern Europe and the north of Africa, where it is an occupant of waste ground and hedges, but still rare in our gardens.

CORNUS.

CORNUS ALBA.--White-fruited Dogwood. Siberia, 1741. This is a native of northern Asia and Siberia, not of America as Loudon stated. For the slender, red-barked branches and white or creamy flowers, this species is well worthy of notice, while the white fruit renders it very distinct and effective. It grows to about 10 feet in height. C. alba Spathi is one of the most ornamental of shrubs bearing coloured leaves, these in spring being of a beautiful bronzy tint, and changing towards summer to a mixture of gold and green, or rather an irregular margin of deep gold surrounds each leaf. It was first sent out by the famous Berlin nurseryman whose name it bears. C. alba Gouchaulti is another variegated leaved variety, but has no particular merit, and originated in one of the French nurseries.

C. ALTERNIFOLIA.--North America, 1760. This species is a lover of damp ground, and grows from 20 feet to nearly 30 feet high, with clusters of pale yellow flowers, succeeded by bluish-black berries that render the plant highly ornamental. It is still rare in British gardens.

C. AMOMUM (syn C. sericea).--From the eastern United States. It is a low-growing, damp-loving shrub, with yellowish-white flowers, borne abundantly in small clusters. It grows about 8 feet in height, and has a graceful habit, owing to the long and lithe branches spreading regularly over the ground. The fruit is pale blue, and the bark a conspicuous purple.

C. ASPERIFOLIA is another showy American species, with reddish-brown bark, hairy leaves, of small size, and rather small flowers that are succeeded by pearly-white berries borne on conspicuous reddish stalks.

C. BAILEYI resembles somewhat the better-known C. stolonifera, but it is of more erect habit, is not stoloniferous, has rather woolly leaves, at least on the under side, and bears yellowish-white fruit. It grows in sandy soil, and is a native of Canada.

C. CALIFORNICA (syn C. pubescens) grows fully 10 feet high, with smooth branches, hairy branchlets, and cymes of pretty white flowers, succeeded by white fruit. It occurs from southern California to British Columbia.

C. CANADENSIS.--Dwarf Cornel or Birchberry. Canada, 1774. This is of herbaceous growth, and remarkable for the large cream-coloured flower bracts, and showy red fruit.

C. CANDIDISSIMA (syn C. paniculata) is a beautiful American species, with panicled clusters of almost pure white flowers, that are succeeded by pale blue fruit. It is a small growing tree, with narrow, pointed leaves, and greyish coloured, smooth bark. Like many of its fellows, this species likes rather moist ground.

C. CIRCINATA, from the eastern United States, is readily distinguished by its large, round leaves, these sometimes measuring 6 inches long by 3-1/2 inches wide. The yellowish-white flowers are individually small, and succeeded by bright blue fruits, each as large as a pea.

C. CAPITATA (syn Benthamia fragifera).--Nepaul, 1825. An evergreen shrub, with oblong, light green leaves and terminal inconspicuous greenish flowers, surrounded by an involucre of four large, pinky-yellow bracts. It is this latter that renders the shrub so very conspicuous when in full flower. Unfortunately, the Benthamia is not hardy throughout the country, the south and west of England, especially Cornwall, and the southern parts of Ireland being the favoured spots where this handsome shrub or small growing tree--for in Cornwall it has attained to fully 45 feet in height, and in Cork nearly 30 feet--may be found in a really thriving condition. Around London it does well enough for a time, but with severe frost it gets cut back to the ground, and though it quickly recovers and grows rapidly afterwards, before it is large enough to flower freely it usually suffers again. The fruits are as large and resemble Strawberries, and of a rich scarlet or reddish hue, and though ripe in October they frequently remain on the trees throughout the winter. Both for its flowers and fruit, this Nepaul shrub-tree is well worthy of a great amount of trouble to get it established in a cosy corner of the garden. Rich, well-drained loam is all it wants, while propagation by seed is readily effected.

C. FLORIDA, the Florida Dogwood, is not always very satisfactory when grown in this country, our climate in some way or other being unsuitable for its perfect development. It is a handsome shrub or small-growing tree, with small flowers surrounded by a large and conspicuous white involucre. The leaves are ovate-oblong, and pubescent on the undersides. It is a valuable as well as ornamental little tree, and is worthy of a great amount of coddling and coaxing to get it established.

C. KOUSA (syn Benthamia japonica).--Japan. This is a very distinct and beautiful flowering shrub. Flowers very small individually, but borne in large clusters, and yellow, the showy part being the four large, pure white bracts which subtend each cluster of blossoms, much like those in Cornus florida, only the bracts are more pointed than those of the latter species. Being quite hardy, and a plant of great interest and beauty, this little known Cornus is sure to be widely planted when better known.

C. MACROPHYLLA (syn C. brachypoda).--Himalayas, China and Japan, 1827. This is an exceedingly handsome species, of tabulated appearance, occasioned by the branches being arranged almost horizontally. The leaves are of large size, elliptic-ovate, and are remarkable for their autumnal tints. The elder-like flowers appear in June. They are pure white and arranged in large cymes. C. macrophylla variegata is a distinct and very ornamental form of the above, in which the leaf margins are bordered with white.

C. MAS.--Cornelian Cherry. Austria, 1596. One of our earliest flowering trees, the clusters of yellow blooms being produced in mild seasons by the middle of February. It is not at all fastidious about soil, thriving well in that of very opposite description. It deserves to be extensively cultivated, if only for the profusion of brightly-tinted flowers, which completely cover the shoots before the leaves have appeared. C. Mas aurea-elegantissima, the tricolor-leaved Dogwood, is a strikingly ornamental shrub, with green leaves encircled with a golden band, the whole being suffused with a faint pinky tinge. It is of more slender growth than the species, and a very desirable acquisition to any collection of hardy ornamental shrubs. C. Mas argenteo-variegata is another pretty shrub, the leaves being margined with clear white.

C. NUTTALLII grows to fully 50 feet in height, and is one of the most beautiful of the Oregon and Californian forest trees. The flower bracts are of large size, often 6 inches across, the individual bracts being broad and white, and fully 2-1/2 inches long.

C. OFFICINALIS is a Japanese species, that is, however, quite hardy in this country, and nearly resembles the better known C. Mas, but from which it may at once be known by the tufts of brownish hairs that are present in the axils of the principal leaf veins.

C. STOLONIFERA.--Red Osier Dogwood. North America, 1741. This has rather inconspicuous flowers, that are succeeded by whitish fruit, and is of greatest value for the ruddy tint of the young shoots. It grows fully 6 feet high, and increases rapidly by underground suckers. The species is quite hardy.

C. TARTARICA (syn C. siberica).--Siberia, 1824. This has much brighter coloured bark, and is of neater and dwarfer habit, than the typical C. alba. It is a very beautiful and valuable shrub, of which there is a variegated leaved form.

COROKIA.

COROKIA COTONEASTER.--New Zealand, 1876. A curious, dwarf-growing shrub, with small, bright yellow, starry flowers produced in June. The hardiness of the shrub is rather doubtful.

CORONILLA.

CORONILLA EMERUS.--Scorpion Senna. France, 1596. This shrub, a native of the middle and southern parts of Europe, forms an elegant loose bush about 5 feet high, with smooth, pinnate, sub-evergreen leaves, and Pea-shaped flowers, that are reddish in the bud state, but bright yellow when fully expanded. It is an elegant plant, and on account of its bearing hard cutting back, is well suited for ornamental hedge formation; but however used the effect is good, the distinct foliage and showy flowers making it a general favourite with planters. It will thrive in very poor soil, but prefers a light rich loam.

CORYLOPSIS.

CORYLOPSIS HIMALAYANA.--E. Himalayas, 1879. This is a stronger growing species than C. pauciflora and C. spicata, with large leaves averaging 4 inches long, that are light green above and silky on the under sides. The parallel veins of the leaves are very pronounced, while the leaf-stalks, as indeed the young twigs too, are covered with a hairy pubescence.

C. PAUCIFLORA is readily distinguished from the former by its more slender growth, smaller leaves, and fewer flowered spikes. Flowers primrose-yellow.

C. SPICATA.--Japan, 1864. This Japanese shrub is of very distinct appearance, having leaves like those of our common Hazel, and drooping spikes of showy-yellowish, fragrant flowers that are produced before the leaves. There is a variegated form in cultivation.

The various species of Corylopsis are very ornamental garden plants, and to be recommended, on account of their early flowering, for prominent positions in the shrubbery or by the woodland walk. Light, rich loam seems to suit them well.

CORYLUS.

CORYLUS AVELLANA PURPUREA.--Purple Hazel. This has large leaves of a rich purple colour, resembling those of the purple Beech, and is a very distinct plant for the shrubbery border. Should be cut down annually if large leaves are desired.

C. COLURNA.--Constantinople Hazel. Turkey, 1665. This is the largest and most ornamental of the family, and is mentioned here on account of the showy catkins with which the tree is usually well supplied. When thickly produced, as they usually are on established specimens, these long catkins have a most effective and pleasing appearance, and tend to render the tree one of the most distinct in cultivation. Under favourable circumstances, such as when growing in a sweet and rather rich brown loam, it attains to fully 60 feet in height, and of a neat shape, from the branches being arranged horizontally, or nearly so. Even in a young state the Constantinople Hazel is readily distinguished from the common English species, by the softer and more angular leaves, and by the whitish bark which comes off in long strips. The stipules, too, form an unerring guide to its identity, they being long, linear, and recurved.

COTONEASTER.

COTONEASTER BACILLARIS.--Nepaul, 1841. A large-growing species, and one
of the few members of the family that is more ornamental in flower than in fruit. It is of bold, portly, upright growth, and sends up shoots from the base of the plant. The pretty white flowers are borne in clusters for some distance along the slender shoots, and have a very effective and pleasing appearance; indeed, the upper portion of the plant has the appearance of a mass of white blossoms.

C. FRIGIDA.--Nepaul, 1824. The species forms a large shrub or low tree with oblong, elliptical, sub-evergreen leaves. The flowers are white and borne in large corymbs, which are followed by scarlet berries in September.

C. MICROPHYLLA.--Small-leaved Cotoneaster. Nepaul, 1825. This is, from a flowering point of view, probably the most useful of any member of this rather large genus. Its numerous pretty white flowers, dark, almost Yew-green leaves, and abundance of the showiest red berries in winter, will ever make this dwarf, clambering plant a favourite with those who are at all interested in beautiful shrubs. All, or nearly all, the species of Cotoneaster are remarkable and highly valued for their showy berries, but, except the above, and perhaps C. buxifolia (Box-leaved Cotoneaster), few others are worthy of consideration from a purely flowering point of view.

C. SIMONSII.--Khasia, 1868. The stems of this species usually grow from 4 feet to 6 feet high, with sub-erect habit. The leaves are roundly-elliptic and slightly silky beneath. The small flowers are succeeded by a profusion of scarlet berries that ripen in autumn. This is generally considered the best for garden purposes.

CRATAEGUS.

CRATAEGUS AZAROLUS.--South Europe, 1640. This is a very vigorous-growing species, with a wide, spreading head of rather upright-growing branches. The flowers are showy and the fruit large and of a pleasing red colour.

C. AZAROLUS ARONIA (syn C. Aronia).--Aronia Thorn. South Europe, 1810. This tree attains to a height of 20 feet, has deeply lobed leaves that are wedge-shaped at the base, and slightly pubescent on the under sides. The flowers, which usually are at their best in June, are white and showy, and succeeded by large yellow fruit. Generally the Aronia Thorn forms a rather upright and branchy specimen of neat proportions, and when studded with its milk-white flowers may be included amongst the most distinct and ornamental of the family.

C. COCCINEA.--Scarlet-fruited Thorn. North America, 1683. If only for its lovely white flowers, with bright, pinky anthers, it is well worthy of a place even in a selection of ornamental flowering trees and shrubs. It is, however, rendered doubly valuable in that the cordate-ovate leaves turn of a warm brick colour in the autumn, while the fruit, and which is usually produced abundantly, is of the brightest red.

C. COCCINEA MACRANTHA.--North America, 1819. This bears some resemblance
to the Cockspur Thorn, but has very long, curved spines--longer, perhaps,
than those of any other species.

C. CORDATA is one of the latest flowering species, in which respect it
is even more hardy than the well-known C. tanace-tifolia. It forms a
small compact tree, of neat and regular outline, with dark green
shining leaves, and berries about the same size as those of the common
species, and deep red.

C. CRUS-GALLI.--Cockspur Thorn. North America, 1691. This has large
and showy white flowers that are succeeded by deep red berries. It is
readily distinguished by the long, curved spines with which the whole
tree is beset. Of this species there are numerous worthy forms,
including C. Crus-galli Carrierii, which opens at first white, and
then turns a showy flesh colour; C. Crus-galli Layi, C. Crus-galli
splendens, C. Crus-galli prunifolia, C. Crus-galli pyracanthifolia, and
C. Crus-galli salicifolia, all forms of great beauty--whether for their
foliage, or beautiful and usually plentifully-produced flowers.

C. DOUGLASII.--North America, 1830. This is peculiar in having dark
purple or almost black fruit. It is of stout growth, often reaching to
20 feet in height, and belongs to the early-flowering section.

C. NIGRA (syn C. Celsiana).--A tree 20 feet high, with stout branches,
and downy, spineless shoots. Leaves large, ovate-acute, deeply incised,
glossy green above and downy beneath. Flowers large and fragrant, pure
white, and produced in close heads in June. Fruit large, oval, downy,
and yellow when fully ripe. A native of Sicily, and known under the
names of C. incisa and C. Leeana. This species must not be confused
with a variety of our common Thorn bearing a similar name.

C. OXYACANTHA.--Common Hawthorn. This is, perhaps, the most ornamental species in cultivation, and certainly the commonest. The common wild species needs no description, the fragrant flowers varying in colour from pure white to pink, being produced in the richest profusion. Under cultivation, however, it has produced some very distinct and desirable forms, far superior to the parent, including amongst others those with double-white, pink, and scarlet flowers.

C. OXYACANTHA PUNICEA flore-pleno (Paul's double-scarlet Thorn), is one of, if not the handsomest variety, with large double flowers that are of the richest crimson. Other good flowering kinds include C. Oxyacantha praecox (Glastonbury Thorn); C. Oxyacantha Oliveriana; C. Oxyacantha punicea, with deep scarlet flowers; C. Oxyacantha rosea, rose-coloured and abundantly-produced flowers; C. Oxyacantha foliis aureis, with yellow fruit; C. Oxyacantha laciniata, cut leaves; C. Oxyacantha multiplex, double-white flowers; C. Oxyacantha foliis argenteis, having silvery-variegated leaves: C. Oxyacantha pendula, of semi-weeping habit; C. Oxyacantha stricta, with an upright and stiff habit of growth; C. Oxyacantha Leeana, a good form; and C. Oxyacantha leucocarpa.

C. PARVIFOLIA.--North America, 1704. This is a miniature Thorn, of slow growth, with leaves about an inch long, and solitary pure-white flowers of large size. The flowers open late in the season, and are succeeded by yellowish-green fruit.

C. PYRACANTHA.--Fiery Thorn. South Europe, 1629. This is a very distinct species, with lanceolate serrated leaves, and pinkish or nearly white flowers. The berries of this species are, however, the principal attraction, being orange-scarlet, and produced in dense clusters. C. Pyracantha crenulata and C. Pyracantha Lelandi are worthy varieties of the above, the latter especially being one of the most ornamental-berried shrubs in cultivation.

C. TANACETIFOLIA.--Tansy-leaved Thorn. Greece, 1789. This is a very late-flowering species, and remarkable for its Tansy-like foliage. It is of unusually free growth, and in almost any class of soil, and is undoubtedly, in so far at least as neatly divided leaves and wealth of fruit are concerned, one of the most distinct and desirable species of Thorn.

Other good species and varieties that may just be mentioned as being worthy of cultivation are C. apiifolia, C. Crus-galli horrida, C. orientalis, and C. tomentosum (syn C. punctata). To a lesser or greater extent, the various species and varieties of Thorn are of great value for the wealth and beauty of flowers they produce, but the above are, perhaps, the most desirable in that particular respect. They are all of free growth, and, except in waterlogged soils, thrive well and flower freely.

CYTISUS.

CYTISUS ALBUS.--White Spanish Broom. Portugal, 1752. This is a large-growing shrub of often 10 feet in height, with wiry, somewhat straggling branches, and remarkable for the wealth of pure-white flowers it produces. In May and June, if favourably situated, every branch is wreathed with small white flowers, and often to such an extent that at a short distance away the plant looks like a sheet of white. Being perfectly hardy and of very free growth in any light soil, and abundantly floriferous, this handsome shrub is one of particular value in ornamental planting. By placing three or five plants in clump-fashion, the beauty of this Broom is greatly enhanced.

C. ALDUS INCARNATUS (syn C. incarnatus) resembles C. purpureus in its leaves and general appearance, but it is of larger growth. The flowers, which are at their best in May, are of a vinous-rose colour, and produced plentifully.

C. BIFLORUS (syn C. elongatus).--Hungary, 1804. This is a dwarf, spreading, twiggy bush, of fully a yard high. Leaves trifoliolate, clothed beneath with closely adpressed hairs, and bright yellow, somewhat tubular flowers, usually produced in fours.

C. DECUMBENS.--A charming alpine species, of low, spreading growth, bright-green three-parted leaves, and bearing axillary bunches of large yellow, brownish-purple tinted flowers. A native of the French and Italian Alps, and quite hardy.

C. NIGRICANS.--Austria, 1730. Another beautiful species, with long, erect racemes of golden-yellow flowers, and one whose general hardihood is undoubted. On its own roots, and allowed to roam at will, this pretty, small-growing Broom is of far greater interest than when it is grafted mop-high on a Laburnum stem, and pruned into artificial shapes, as is, unfortunately, too often the case.

C. PURPUREUS.--Purple Broom. Austria, 1792. Alow, spreading shrub, with long wiry shoots, clothed with neat trifoliolate leaves, and bearing an abundance of its purple, Pea-shaped flowers. There is a white-flowered form, C. purpureus albus, and another named C. purpureus ratis-bonensis, with pretty yellow flowers, produced on long and slender shoots.

C. SCOPARIUS.--Yellow Broom. This is a well-known native shrub, with silky, angular branches, and bright yellow flowers in summer. There are several varieties, but the most remarkable and handsome is C. scoparius Andreanus, in which the wings of the flowers are of a rich golden brown. It is one of the showiest shrubs in cultivation.

For ornamental planting the above are about the best forms of Broom, but others might include C. austriacus, C. Ardoini, and C. capitatus, the latter being unusually hardy, and bearing dense heads of flowers. In so far as soil is concerned, the Brooms are readily accommodated, while either from seeds or cuttings they are easily propagated.

DABOECIA.

DABOECIA POLIFOLIA (syn Menziesia polifolia).--St. Dabeoc's Heath. South Western Europe, Ireland and the Azores. A dwarf, and rather straggling, viscid shrub, with linear-ovate leaves that are silvery beneath. The flowers are pink, and abundantly produced. D. polifolia alba has white flowers; and D. polifolia atro-purpurea, purplish flowers.

DANAE.

DANAE LAURUS (syn D. racemosa and *Ruscus racemosus*).--Alexandrian Laurel. A native of Portugal (1739), with glossy-green leaf substitutes, and racemes of small, not very showy, greenish-yellow flowers.

DAPHNE.

DAPHNE ALPINA.--Italy, 1759. A deciduous species, which has white or rosy-white, sweet-scented flowers. It is a pretty, but rare shrub, that grows well in light sandy leaf soil.

D. ALTAICA.--Siberia, 1796. Though rare in gardens, this is a pretty and neat-foliaged species, and bears white flowers in abundance. It wants a warm corner and dry soil.

D. BLAGAYANA.--Styria, 1872. This is still rare in cultivation, but it is a very desirable species, bearing ivory-white highly-fragrant flowers. For the alpine garden it is particularly suitable, and though growing rather slowly thrives well in good light soil.

D. CHAMPIONI
(syn D. Fortunei), from China, is a rare and pretty species, bearing lilac flowers in winter, and whilst the shrub is leafless. It does best in a warm situation, such as planted against a wall facing south.

D. CNEORUM.--Garland Flower. South Europe, 1752. This is a charming rock shrub, of dwarf, trailing habit, with small glossy-green leaves, and dense clusters of deep pink, deliciously-fragrant flowers.

D. FIONIANA is of neat growth, with small, glossy, dark leaves, and pale rose-coloured flowers. Its sturdy, dwarf habit, constant verdure, and pretty sweet-scented flowers, should make this species a favourite with cultivators. Known also as D. hyemalis.

D. GENKWA.--Japanese Lilac. Japan, 1866. This is a rare and beautiful species, of recent introduction, with large lilac-tinted, sweetly-scently flowers.

D. LAUREOLA.--Spurge Laurel. This is not, in so far at least as flowers are concerned, a showy species, but the ample foliage and sturdy habit of the plant will always render this native species of value for the shrubbery. It is of value, too, as growing and flowering freely in the shade. The flowers are sweetly-scented and of a greenish-yellow colour, and appear about February.

D. MEZEREUM.--The Mezereon. Europe (England). One of the commonest and
most popular of hardy garden shrubs. It is of stout, strict growth, and

produces clusters of pinky, rose, or purplish flowers before winter is past, and while the branches are yet leafless. Few perfectly hardy flowering shrubs are so popular as the Mezereon, and rightly so, for a more beautiful plant could not be mentioned, wreathed as every branch is, and almost back to the main stem, with the showiest of flowers. It likes good, rich, dampish soil, and delights to grow in a quiet, shady nook, or even beneath the spread of our larger forest trees. There are several very distinct varieties, of which the white-flowered D. Mezereum flore albo is one of the most valuable. The fruit of this variety is bright golden-yellow. D. Mezereum autumnale and D. Mezereum atro-rubrum are likewise interesting and beautiful forms.

D. PETRAEA (syn D. rupestris).--Rock Daphne. Tyrol. This is quite hardy in the more sheltered corners of the rock garden, with neat, shining foliage and pretty rosy flowers, produced so thickly all over the plant as almost to hide the foliage from view. At Kew it thrives well in peaty loam and limestone, and although it does not increase very quickly is yet happy and contented. It is a charming rock shrub.

D. PONTICA.--Pontic Daphne. Asia Minor, 1759. This is much like D. lauriola, but has shorter and more oval leaves, and the flowers, instead of being borne in fives like that species, are produced in pairs. They are also of a richer yellow, and more sweetly scented.

D. SERICEA (syn D. collina).--Italy and Asia Minor, 1820. This forms a bush fully 2 feet high, with evergreen, oblong, shining leaves, and clusters of rose-coloured flowers that are pleasantly scented. It is quite hardy, and an interesting species that is well worthy of more extended culture. There is a variety of this with broader foliage than the species, and named D. sericea latifolia (syn D. collina latifolia).

DAPHNIPHYLLUM.

DAPHNIPHYLLUM GLAUCESCENS.--East Indies, Java and Corea. A handsome
Japanese shrub that will be valued for its neat Rhododendron-like foliage, compact habit of growth, and for the conspicuous bark which is of a warm reddish hue. The leaves are large and elliptic, six inches long, and are rendered strangely conspicuous from the foot-stalks and midrib being dull crimson, this affording a striking contrast to the delicate green of the leaves. It grows freely in light sandy peat. There are two well-marked forms, one named D. glaucescens viridis, in which the red markings of the leaves are absent; and D. glaucescens jezoensis, a pretty and uncommon variety.

DESFONTAINEA.

DESFONTAINEA SPINOSA.--Andes from Chili to New Grenada, 1853. This is a desirable shrub, and one that is perfectly hardy in most parts of the country. It is a charming shrub of bold, bushy habit, with prickly holly-like foliage, and scarlet and yellow, trumpet-shaped pendent flowers, borne in quantity. The shelter of a wall favours the growth and flowering of this handsome shrub, but it also succeeds well in the open if planted in rich, light soil, and in positions that are not exposed to cold and cutting winds.

DEUTZIA.

DEUTZIA CRENATA (syn D. scabra and ***D. Fortunei***).--Japan 1863. This is of stout, bushy growth, often reaching a height of 8 feet, and lateral spread of nearly as much. The ovate-lanceolate leaves are rough to the touch, and its slender, but wiry stems, are wreathed for a considerable distance along with racemes of pure white flowers. It is a very distinct shrub, of noble port, and when in full flower is certainly one of the most ornamental of hardy shrubs. The double-flowered form, D. crenata flore-pleno, is one of the prettiest flowering shrubs in cultivation, the wealth of double flowers, not white as in the species, but tinged with reddish-purple being highly attractive. D. crenata, Pride of Rochester, is another form with double-white flowers, and a most distinct and beautiful shrub. Two other very beautiful varieties are those known as D. crenata Watererii and D. crenata Wellsii.

D. GRACILIS is a somewhat tender shrub of fully 18 inches high, with smooth leaves and pure-white flowers produced in the greatest freedom. It does well in warm, sheltered sites, but is most frequently seen as a greenhouse plant. A native of Japan.

DIERVILLA.

DIERVILLA FLORIBUNDA (syn D. multiflora and *Weigelia floribunda*), from Japan, 1864, has narrow, tubular, purplish-coloured corollas, that are only slightly opened out at the mouth. The Diervillas are valuable decorative shrubs, of free growth in good rich loam, and bearing a great abundance of the showiest of flowers. For shrubbery planting they must ever rank high, the beautiful flowers and rich green ample leafage rendering them distinct and attractive.

D. GRANDIFLORA (syn D. amabilis and *Weigelia amabilis*).--Japan. This is of larger growth than D. rosea, with strongly reticulated leaves, that are prominently veined on the under sides, and much larger, almost white flowers. It is a distinct and worthy species. There are some beautiful varieties of this species, named Isolinae, Van Houttei, and Striata.

D. ROSEA (syn Weigelia rosea).--China, 1844. This is a handsome hardy shrub of small stature, with ovate-lanceolate leaves, and clusters of showy pink, or sometimes white flowers, that are produced in April and May. There are many good varieties of this shrub, of which the following are the most popular:--D. rosea arborescens grandiflora; D. rosea Lavallii, with an abundance of crimson-red flowers; D. rosea Stelzneri, with an abundance of deep red flowers; D. rosea hortensis nivea, large foliage, and large, pure-white flowers; D. rosea candida, much like the latter, but bearing pure-white flowers; and D. rosea Looymansii aurea has beautiful golden leaves.

DISCARIA.

DISCARIA LONGISPINA.--This is at once a curious and beautiful shrub, of low, creeping growth, and poorly furnished with leaves, which, however, are amply made up for by the deep green of the shoots and stems, and which give to the plant almost the appearance of an evergreen. The flowers, which are bell-shaped and white, are almost lavishly produced, and as they last for a very long time, with only the pure white assuming a pinky tinge when subjected to excessive sunshine, the value of the shrub is still further enhanced. For planting against a mound of rock this scrambling shrub is of value, but the position should not be exposed to cold winds, for the plant is somewhat tender. From South America, and allied to the better known Colletias.

D. SERRATIFOLIA (syn Colletia serratifolia), is even a handsomer plant than the former, with minute serrated foliage, and sheets of small white flowers in June.

DIOSPYROS.

DIOSPYROS KAKI COSTATA.--The Date Plum. China, 1789. Fruit as big as a small apple; leaves leathery, entire, and broadly ovate; flowers and fruits in this country when afforded the protection of a wall. The fruit is superior to that of D. virginiana (Persimmon).

D. LOTUS, the common Date Plum, is a European species, with purplish flowers, and oblong leaves that are reddish on the under sides. Both species want a light, warm soil, and sheltered situation.

D. VIRGINIANA.--The Persimmon, or Virginian Date Plum. North America, 1629. A small-growing tree, with coriaceous leaves, and greenish-yellow flowers. In southern situations and by the seaside it is perfectly hardy, and succeeds well, but in other districts it is rather tender. The fruit is edible, yellow in colour, and about an inch in diameter.

DIRCA.

DIRCA PALUSTRIS.--Leather Wood. North America, 1750. A much-branched bush, of quite a tree-like character, but rarely more than 3 feet high. To the Daphnes it is nearly allied, and is close in resemblance; but there is a curious yellowish hue pervading the whole plant. The flowers are produced on the naked shoots in April, and are rendered conspicuous by reason of the pendent yellow stamens. They are borne in terminal clusters of three or four together. It delights to grow in a cool, moist soil, indeed it is only when so situated that the Leather Wood can be seen in a really thriving condition.

DRIMYS.

DRIMYS AROMATICA (syn Tasmannia aromatica).--Tasmanian Pepper Plant. Tasmania, 1843. This is, if we might say so, a more refined plant than D. Winteri, with smaller and narrower leaves, and smaller flowers. The plant, too, has altogether a faint reddish tinge, and is of upright growth. A native of Tasmania, and called by the natives the Pepper Plant, the fruit being used as a substitute for that condiment. Like the other species the present plant is only hardy in warm, maritime places, and when afforded the protection of a wall.

D. WINTERI (syn Winter a aromatica).--Winter's Bark. South America, 1827. The fine evergreen character is the chief attraction of this American shrub, so far at least as garden ornamentation is concerned. With some persons even the greenish-white flowers are held in esteem, and it cannot be denied that a well flowered plant has its own attractions. The long, narrow leaves are pale green above and glaucous beneath, and make the shrub of interest, both on account of their evergreen nature and brightness of tint. Unfortunately it is not very hardy, requiring even in southern England a sunny wall to do it justice.

ELAEAGNUS.

ELAEAGNUS ARGENTEA.--Silver Berry. North America, 1813. A spreading shrub 8 feet or 10 feet high, with lanceolate leaves clothed with silvery scales. The flowers are axillary and clustered, and are succeeded by pretty, silvery-ribbed berries.

E. GLABRA (syn E. reflexus).--From Japan. This is one of the handsomest species, forming bushes of delightful green, leathery leaves, and with a neat and rather compact habit of growth. It grows with great freedom when planted in light, sandy soil, big globose bushes being the result of a few years' growth. Being perfectly hardy it is to be recommended if only for the ample leathery, deep green foliage. The flowers are inconspicuous. There is a form having the leaves margined with pale yellow, and known under the name of E. glabra variegata.

E. LONGIPES (syn E. edulis and *E. crisp a*).--Japan, 1873. This species, is also worthy of culture, whether for the ornamental flowers or fruit. It is a shrub 6 feet high, bearing an abundance of spotted, oval red berries on long footstalks. Quite hardy.

E. MACROPHYLLA.--Japan. This is of robust growth, with handsome, dark green leaves, and purplish branch tips. The leaves are thick of texture, often fully 3 inches long, glossy-green above, and silvery beneath. The latter is all the more remarkable, as the leaves have the habit of curling up their edges, and thus revealing the light, silvery tint of the under sides. It thrives well in light, sandy peat, and may be relied upon as one of the hardiest of shrubs.

E. ROTUNDIFOLIA.--An interesting and perfectly hardy species, growing about five feet high, and remarkable for the great wealth of pretty scarlet and amber-coloured berries. The flowers are not very showy, but this is made up by the beautiful silvery leaves, most pronounced on the under sides, and wealth of fruit, which hangs on long stalks like Cherries.

Other species of less interest are E. pungens, of which there is a variegated variety; E. Simoni, a neat Chinese shrub; and E. latifolia, of good habit and with large leaves. The various species and varieties of Elaeagnus may all be cultivated in light, free soil, and from experiments that were recently made, they have been found of great value for planting by the seaside. They are popularly known as the Wild

Olives and Evergreen Oleasters.

EMBOTHRIUM.

EMBOTHRIUM COCCINEUM.--Fire Bush. South America, 1851. This is a beautiful shrub, of tall growth, with flowers of great interest and beauty. Except in warm and favoured situations, it is not very hardy, and should always be grown as a wall plant. The fiery scarlet, orange-tinted flowers, resembling somewhat those of the Honeysuckle, are very beautiful by the first weeks of May. It grows to about 6 feet in height in southern England, and is, when in full flower, a shrub of unusual beauty.

EPHEDRA.

EPHEDRA VULGARIS (syn Ephedra monastachya), from Siberia, 1772, is a half-hardy shrub of trailing habit, with inconspicuous flowers. Thriving in very poor soil, or on rocky situations, is the only reason why it is introduced here.

EPIGAEA.

EPIGAEA REPENS.--Ground Laurel, or New England Mayflower. Northern United States, 1736. This is, perhaps, in so far as stature is concerned, hardly worthy of a place in our list, yet it is such a pretty and useful shrub, though rarely rising more than 6 inches from the ground, that we cannot well pass it over. For planting beneath Pine or other trees, where it can spread about at will, this prostrate shrub is most at home. There it enlivens the spot with its pretty evergreen foliage, and sweet-scented, white or pinky flowers. It is quite hardy.

ERCILLA.

ERCILLA SPICATA (syn Bridgesia spicata).--Chili, 1840. A small-growing, half-climbing shrub, with leathery, deep green leaves, and inconspicuous flowers. Hailing from Chili, it is not very hardy, but given the protection of a wall, or planted against a tree-stump, it soon forms a neat mass of evergreen foliage.

ERICA.

ERICA CARNEA.--South Europe, 1763. This is one of the most beautiful and desirable of hardy Heaths, on account of the richly-coloured flowers and early season at which they are produced. In the typical species the flowers are pink or flesh-coloured, and produced in January and February. It is a dwarf, compact growing species, with bright green foliage. There is a form with pure white flowers, named E. carnea alba, or E. herbacea, but although distinct and beautiful, it is not of so robust growth as the parent.

E. CILIARIS.--A pretty native species, with ciliate glandular leaves, and racemes of highly-coloured, rosy flowers. Found in Dorsetshire and Cornwall.

E. CINEREA,--Gray-leaved Heath. In this species, also a native of Britain, the flowers are of a reddish-purple colour, and borne in dense terminal racemes. There are numerous varieties, including a white-flowered E. cinerea alba; E. cinerea atro-purpurea, bearing dark purple flowers; E. cinerea atro-sanguinea, dark red flowers; E. cinerea coccinea, scarlet; E. cinerea purpurea, purple flowers; and E. cinerea rosea, with deep rose-coloured flowers.

E. MEDITERRANEA.--Mediterranean Heath. Portugal, 1648. This is a robust-growing species, of rather erect habit, and often attaining to fully a yard in height. Flowers abundantly produced, and of a pretty pinky hue. Of this there are several varieties, the following being best known: E. mediterranea hibernica, found in Ireland; E. mediterranea alba, with white flowers; E. mediterranea nana, of very dwarf growth; and E. mediterranea rubra, with showy, deep red flowers.

E. SCOPARIA and E. ERECTA are desirable species, the former bearing greenish flowers, and the latter of decidedly upright growth.

E. TETRALIX.--Cross-leaved Heath. A native species of low, and bushy growth, with close umbels or terminal clusters of pretty pinky flowers. The varieties of this most worthy of notice are E. Tetralix alba, white flowered; E. Tetralix Mackiana, crimson flowered; E. Tetralix rubra, deep red flowers; and E. Tetralixbicolor, with parti-coloured flowers.

E. VAGANS..--Cornish Heath. A native species, bearing pinky-white flowers, but there are forms with white and red flowers, named E. vagans alba and E. vagans rubra.

The various kinds of Heath succeed best either in peaty soil, or that composed for the greater part of light, sandy loam, but many will grow and flower freely if planted in rich yellow loam. They are very desirable plants, either for bed formation, for rockwork ornamentation, or for planting around the shrubbery margins. Propagation is effected either by cuttings or sub-divisions, but seedlings of several species spring up freely under favourable conditions.

ESCALLONIA.

ESCALLONIA FLORIBUNDA (syn E. montevideusis).--New Grenada, 1827. This is one of the handsomest species, bearing long, arching clusters of white flowers. It is a very desirable shrub for wall or lattice-work covering, against which it grows rapidly, and soon forms an object of great beauty by reason of its neat foliage and graceful habit, as also wealth of pretty flowers.

E. ILLINATA.--Chili, 1830. This should also be included, it being a handsome and pretty-flowered plant.

E. MACRANTHA.--Chiloe, 1848. This is a general favourite in English gardens, where it succeeds well, but especially in maritime parts of the country. It is of stout growth, 6 feet or more in height, of spreading habit, and with elliptical, serrulated, bright green leaves, and clusters of crimson-red flowers produced in summer. For wall-covering this is an almost invaluable shrub, although it succeeds well as a standard in all but the colder parts of the country. Any free, open soil suits it well, but thorough drainage must be attended to. There are several very distinct and good varieties, such as E. macrantha sanguinea, with flowers deeper in colour than those of the parent plant; and E. macrantha Ingrami, a profuse-blooming and very desirable form.

E. PHILLIPIANA.--Valdivia, 1873. When seen as a standard bush, and loaded with its myriads of tiny white flowers, this must rank amongst the handsomest members of the family. It is very hardy, and retains its foliage throughout the winter. The hybrid forms, E. exoniensis and E. leucantha, deserve recognition, the latter even as late as November being laden with its small spikes of pretty white flowers, which contrast nicely with the neat, evergreen foliage.

E. PTEROCLADON.--Patagonia, 1854. This is remarkable for the curiously-winged branches, which give to the shrub a rather peculiar and distinct appearance. The freely-produced flowers are white or pink.

E. RUBRA.--Chili, 1827. This has less handsome leaves and flowers than the above, but it is, all the same, a beautiful plant. The flowers vary a good deal in depth of colouring, and may be seen of all tints between pure white and red.

The Escallonias are all of very free growth in any light, warm, sandy, and well-drained soil, and are readily propagated.

EUCRYPHIA.

EUCRYPHIA PINNATIFOLIA.--Chili, 1880. This shrub, is as yet rare in cultivation, and is not suited for the colder or more exposed parts of the country. It is, however, a singularly distinct and beautiful shrub, with deep glossy-green, pinnate foliage, and bearing large, pure white flowers, that are rendered all the more conspicuous by the golden-yellow anthers. As an ornamental shrub it is well worthy of cultivation. In so far as its hardihood in this climate has to do, it may be mentioned that in various parts of England and Ireland it has stood in the open ground unharmed for several years back. Light, sandy, well drained peat would seem to meet with its requirements.

EUONYMUS.

EUONYMUS AMERICANA.--American Spindle Tree. North America, 1686. This is a deciduous or semi-evergreen shrub, of about 6 feet in height, found over a wide area in Canada and the United States. It is of partially erect growth, with long and lithe branches, covered with pleasing light green bark. Flowers appearing in June, and succeeded by rough, warted, brilliant scarlet capsules, which are particularly showy and attractive. It likes a shady situation, and rich, rather damp soil.

E. EUROPAEUS.--West Asia, Europe (Britain), &c. An indigenous species, rarely exceeding 6 feet in height, and rendered very effective in autumn by reason of the pale scarlet fruit, which, when fully ripe, and having split open, reveals the orange-coloured arils of the seeds. It, too, delights to grow in the shade.

E. FIMBRIATUS, Japan and India, and its handsome variegated form, E. fimbriatus foliis variegatus et argenteo maculatus, are rather too tender for cultivation in this country, even in southern districts, and where afforded wall protection. E. verrucosus and E. atropurpureus are also worthy of cultivation.

E. LATIFOLIUS.--Broad-leaved Spindle Tree. A European species (1730), deciduous, and growing from 10 feet to sometimes fully 20 feet in height. The leaves are bright, shining green, and much larger than those of our native species. Flowers, purplish-white, appearing in June; the capsules large, deep red, and when open contrasting very effectively with the bright orange arils in which the seeds are enveloped. It is a very distinct and beautiful, small-growing lawn tree, and succeeding, as it does, best in shade is an extra qualification.

FABIANA.

FABIANA IMBRICATA.--Chili, 1838. This is, unfortunately, not hardy in any but the milder maritime parts of England and Ireland. It is a charming shrub of Heather-like appearance, with small, crowded leaves, and pure white flowers produced in May. Planted at the base of a southern wall it does best, and where it thrives it is certainly one of our handsomest half-hardy shrubs.

FATSIA.

FATSIA JAPONICA (syns Aralia japonica and *A. Sieboldii*).--Japan, 1858. This is of no particular value as a flowering shrub, but being hardy in most districts, and having large handsome leaves that impart to it a tropical appearance, it is well worthy of culture. The flowers are ivory-white, and produced in large umbels towards the end of autumn, but our early frosts too often mar their beauty. In this country it grows about 10 feet high, and is usually what is termed "leggy" in appearance, and thrives well in any good loamy soil if fairly dry.

FENDLERA.

FENDLERA RUPICOLA.--Mexico, 1888. A low-growing shrub, peculiar to the dry rocky parts of the United States, particularly the south-western district. It grows about a yard high, and bears a great profusion of bluish-white flowers, that are rendered very conspicuous by reason of the bright yellow stamens. It is the only known species, and is nearly allied to the Saxifrages. Any fairly good garden soil will suit it well, but it wants to be planted where superfluous moisture is quickly carried off.

FORSYTHIA.

FORSYTHIA SUSPENSA (syn F. Fortunei and *F. Sieboldii*).--Japan and China, 1864. A slender-growing shrub, with variable leaves, and long, trailing shoots. The flowers are abundantly produced, are of a beautiful golden tint, and bell-shaped, and being of good substance last for a long time. Either as a wall plant, or for using in some sheltered corner, and where the branches can spread about at will, it forms a very distinct and handsome shrub, and one that is perfectly hardy and quite indifferent as regards the quality of soil in which it is planted. There are several forms of this pretty shrub, but as they do not differ to any great extent from the species, are hardly worthy of consideration.

F. suspensa intermedia is a garden hybrid, 1891.

F. VIRIDISSIMA.--Japan, 1845. This is another desirable species, but it is not comparable in point of beauty with the former. It is usually of strong erect growth, with stout shoots, wreathed with bright yellow flowers towards the end of winter. It is a very beautiful shrub, and a valuable addition to the winter or early spring flowering section.

FOTHERGILLA.

FOTHERGILLA ALNIFOLIA.--North Eastern America, 1765. This is an ungainly habited shrub, of dwarf growth, the branches being somewhat slender and crooked. The flowers are white, sweetly scented, and produced in dense terminal spikes. It is perfectly hardy.

FRAXINUS.

FRAXINUS ORNUS (syn F. argentea, F. rotundifolia, and *Ornus europea*).--Manna Ash. South Europe, 1730. This is a handsome tree, especially when young and vigorous, and by far the most ornamental species in cultivation. For planting in situations where large-growing subjects would be out of place this is a valuable tree, while the wealth of flowers renders it particularly interesting and effective. It rarely exceeds 30 feet in height, with leaves not unlike those of the common Ash, and conspicuous panicles of light, feathery, white petaliferous flowers, produced usually in great abundance all over the tree. Perfectly hardy.

F. Ornus serotina alba and F. Ornus serotina violacea are beautiful seedling forms that were raised in France, and on account of their dwarf habit and profusion of flowers are well worthy of attention. The flowers of the first-named variety are pure white, the stamens having at first yellow anthers, which speedily turn to a rich blackish-brown. The other differs but little, only in the flowers, which are of a distinct greyish-violet hue, while the leaves are of a darker shade of green, and the leaflets longer and narrower.

F. MARIESII.--Northern China, 1880. This is hardy in most parts of the country. The whole tree is quite glabrous except the petioles, which are clothed with a dense pubescence. Flowers pure white, and arranged in large dense panicles.

FREMONTIA.

FREMONTIA CALIFORNICA.--California, 1851. A handsome and deciduous Californian shrub, but scarcely hardy enough for the open air without protection. In Southern England and Ireland, however, it does well, and all the better if planted within the influence of the sea. The large yellow flowers are often about 2 inches across, and produced singly along the branches, while the leaves are large, lobed, and of an enticing shade of green. Planted against a wall, in good dampish loam, it succeeds well.

FUCHSIA.

FUCHSIA MACROSTEMA GLOBOSA (syn F. globosa).--Chili. This is readily recognised by the globose form assumed by the incurved sepals, while the flowers are smaller and less showy than those of F. Riccartoni. Hardihood about similar to the following.

F. RICCARTONI.--This seedling from F. m. globosa is one of the two hardiest varieties, but even this plant, except in warm, maritime districts, is by no means satisfactory. Where it does well it is a shrub of great beauty, and blooms profusely. This species has red, straight sepals, and a purple corolla. In favoured districts it may frequently be seen as much as 12 feet high, and is then during the flowering period an object of great beauty. It originated at Riccarton, near Edinburgh, about 1830.

GARRYA.

GARRYA ELLIPTICA.--California, 1818. This is a handsome shrub, with dark green coreaceous leaves, resembling very nearly those of the Evergreen Oak. The long, tassellated catkins, of a peculiar yellowish-green colour, render the plant one of much interest and beauty. As a wall plant it thrives well, the slight protection thus afforded favouring the growth and expansion of the catkins. For planting in the shrubbery it is also well suited, and where it oft-times attains to a height of 6 feet, and is bushy in proportion. It is well to bear in mind that there are male and female plants of the Garrya, and that the former is the more ornamental. Good rich, well-drained loam will suit this shrub well.

GAULTHERIA.

GAULTHERIA NUMMARIOIDES (syn G. nummulariae and **G. repens**).--Himalayas. This is a neat Alpine species, with small and very dark green leaves. It likes a shady situation and vegetable soil. For planting on the rockwork, amongst tree roots, or beneath the shade of trees, the Gaultherias are particularly suitable. Light, but rich vegetable soil suits them best.

G. PROCUMBENS.--Canada Tea, or Creeping Winter-green. North America, 1762. This is of much smaller growth than the following, rarely rising to a greater height than about half a foot, with lanceolate, serrated leaves, and pendulous axillary clusters of white flowers.

G. SHALLON.--North-west America, 1826. Growing in favourable situations to fully a yard in height, this distinct evergreen shrub, which is fairly common in cultivation, is particularly valuable, as it thrives well under the shade and drip of trees. It is a rambling plant, with ovate-cordate, almost sessile leaves, and bears tiny white flowers that are succeeded by purplish fruit. G. Shallon acutifolia has more sharply pointed leaves than those of the species.

GENISTA.

GENISTA AETNENSIS (syn Spartium aetnensis).--Etna Broom. Sicily and Sardinia, 1816. This is a large-growing species of elegant growth, and remarkable for the abundance of yellow flowers with which it is literally covered in August. Than this South-European Pea-flower, perhaps not another member of the family is more worthy of culture, the neat, elegant habit of growth and profusion of flowers rendering it a plant of particular interest and beauty. It is quite hardy, thrives in any light soil if well drained, and is readily propagated from seed, which it ripens in abundance.

G. ANXANTICA.--Naples, 1818. This is a nearly allied species to our native G. tinctoria, and is of dwarf growth with a rich abundance of golden yellow flowers that are produced towards the end of summer.

G. CINEREA (syn G. ramosissima), from South Europe, is a very beautiful and desirable species, a yard high, and bearing in July slender twigs of the brightest yellow flowers.

G. EPHEDROIDES.--Corsica and Sardinia, 1832. With small and abundantly-produced flowers, this resembles Ephedra, hence its name.

G. GERMANICA.--Germany, 1773. This is a handsome rock garden shrub, of fully 18 inches in height, with arching stems and a plentiful supply of bright flowers during the summer and autumn months.

G. HISPANICA.--South-western Europe, 1759. This species resembles our common Broom, but the branches are not angular. The large, yellow, fragrant flowers appear in July. There is a charming double-flowered variety named G. hispanica flore-pleno.

G. LUSITANICA.--Portugal, 1771. This is remarkable for its opposite branches, is of spiny growth, and one of the earliest to appear in flower.

G. MONOSPERMA.--South Europe, 1690. This has white flowers, and is of value as a seaside shrub, and grows well in almost pure sand. A native of the Mediterranean coast.

G. PILOSA.--Greenweed. Europe (Britain). This is a dense prostrate native species, with bright yellow blossoms produced freely during May and June. A delightful rock shrub, and one that will succeed well almost in pure gravel.

G. PROSTRATA.--Burgundy and Alps of Jura, 1775. A small-growing species suitable for rock gardening, and of spreading bushy growth. Flowers small, but ornamental, and produced in May and June.

G. RADIATA (syn Spartium radiatum).--South Europe, 1758. This is a slender-growing shrub, about 18 inches high, with narrow leaflets, and terminal heads of yellow flowers produced in summer.

G. SAGITTALIS.--South Europe, 1750. With its peculiarly winged and jointed stems, which are of a deep green colour, this is one of the most distinct forms. The flowers are few but pretty, and with the dwarf habit render the plant an excellent subject for rockwork.

G. TINCTORIA.--Dyers' Greenweed. Europe (Britain), North and West Asia. This is a spineless species, and bears a profusion of yellow flowers from July onwards. The double-flowering variety, G. tinctoria flore-pleno, is, in so far as ornamental qualities are concerned, superior to the parent form.

G. TINCTORIA ELATIOR (syn G. elatior) grows to 12 feet in height, is of free, spreading growth, and a very handsome plant. The flowers, which are individually small and yellow, are so thickly produced that the shrub, in late summer, has the appearance of a sheet of gold.

G. TRIANGULARIS (syn G. triquetra).--South Europe, 1815. This is a decidedly good garden plant, and of neat, trailing habit. The stems are three sided, and the flowers golden yellow and plentifully produced. A native of South Europe, and perfectly hardy in almost any position.

The above include most of the hardy Genistas, though G. capitata and G. daurica, both very ornamental kinds, might be added to the list. They are all very hardy, free-flowering shrubs, of simple culture, and succeeding well in any light and rather dry soil.

GLEDITSCHIA.

GLEDITSCHIA TRIACANTHOS.--Honey Locust. United States, 1700. As an ornamental hardy tree this is well worthy the attention of planters, the pinnate and bipinnate foliage being particularly elegant, while the flowers, though individually small, are borne in such quantities of fascicled racemes as to attract notice. The stem and branches are armed with formidable prickles, but there is a form in which the prickles are absent. A native of North America, and readily cultivated in any soil of even fair quality. For town planting it is a valuable tree. There is a good weeping variety named G. triacanthos pendula.

G. SINENSIS (syn G. horrida).--China, 1774. This nearly resembles the latter, and is occasionally to be met with in cultivation in this country.

GORDONIA.

GORDONIA LASIANTHUS.--Loblolly Bay. North America, 1739. A shrub of great beauty, but one that, unfortunately, is rarely to be seen outside the walls of a botanic garden. It is of Camellia-like growth, with large, sweetly fragrant flowers and a good habit of growth.

G. PUBESCENS.--North America, 1774. This is of smaller growth than the latter, rarely exceeding about 6 feet high, with large white flowers that are rendered all the more conspicuous by the tuft of golden stamens. Both species are somewhat tender, although hailing from the coast, swampy grounds of the southern States of North America. Planted in favoured sites, they usually grow freely in light, peaty soil, or that containing a large admixture of decayed leaf soil.

GRABOWSKIA.

GRABOWSKIA BOERHAAVIAEFOLIA.--Peru, 1780. This is occasionally to be
seen in sheltered and favoured gardens, but it is not to be relied upon in other than southern and seaside districts. The plant is of no particular interest to the cultivator, the outline being ungainly, while the pale blue flowers are both dull and uninteresting. It belongs to the Solanum family, and is only worth cultivating as a curiosity. Light, warm soil and a sunny position are necessities in the cultivation of this shrub.

GRISELINIA.

GRISELINIA LITTORALIS.--New Zealand, 1872. This forms a compact bush of moderate size, and is fairly hardy. The leaves are of a light, pleasing green shade, coriaceous, and glossy, and remain on the plant during winter. It is an excellent shrub for the seaside, and, moreover, will succeed well in stiff soils where many other plants would refuse to grow.

GYMNOCLADUS.

GYMNOCLADUS CANADENSIS.--Kentucky Coffee Tree. Canada, 1748. When in full leafage this is a distinct and beautiful tree, the foliage hanging in well-rounded masses, and presenting a pretty effect by reason of the loose and tufted appearance of the masses of finely-divided leaves. Leaves often 3 feet long, bipinnate, and composed of numerous bluish-green leaflets. Flowers white, borne in loose spikes in the beginning of summer, and succeeded by flat, somewhat curved brown pods. It prefers a rich, strong soil or alluvial deposit.

G. CHINENSIS.--Soap Tree. China, 1889. Readily distinguished from the American species by its much smaller and more numerous leaflets, and thicker fruit pod. It is not very hardy in this country unless in the milder sea-side districts. The leaves are used by the Chinese women to wash their hair, hence the popular name of Soap Tree.

HALESIA.

HALESIA DIPTERA (syn H. reticulata).--North America, 1758. This is not so suitable for our climate as H. tetraptera, though in southern parts of the country it forms a neat, healthy bush, and flowers freely. It is distinguished, as the name indicates, by having two wings to the seed vessel, H. tetraptera having four.

H. HISPIDA (syn Pterostyrax hispidum).--Japan, 1875. This is a shrub of perfect hardihood, free growth, and very floriferous. The flowers, which are pure white, and in long racemes, resemble much those of the Snowdrop Tree. Leaves broad and slightly dentated. It is a handsome shrub, of free growth, in light, sandy loam, and quite hardy even when fully exposed.

H. PARVIFLORA has smaller flowers than those of our commonly-cultivated plant.

H. TETRAPTERA.--Snowdrop Tree. North America, 1756. This is a very ornamental tall-growing shrub, of somewhat loose growth, and bearing flowers which resemble, both in size and appearance, those of our common Snowdrop. It is one of the most ornamental of all the small-growing American trees, and richly deserves a place in every collection, on account of the profusion with which the flowers are produced in April and May. They are snow-white, drooping, and produced in lateral fascicles of eight or ten together. It is a native of river banks in North Carolina, and is well suited for cultivation in this country. Light, peaty soil will grow it to perfection.

HALIMODENDRON.

HALIMODENDRON ARGENTEUM (syn Robinia Halimodendron).--Salt tree. A native of Asiatic Russia (1779), having silvery foliage, and pink or purplish-pink flowers, axillary or fascicled. It is a neat and pretty shrub, that is rendered valuable as succeeding well in maritime districts. Quite hardy and of free growth in sandy soil.

HAMAMELIS.

HAMAMELIS JAPONICA.--The Japanese Witch Hazel. Japan, 1862. This is a small species with lemon-yellow flowers. H. japonica arborea is a taller growing variety, with primrose-yellow petals, and a deep claret calyx. The flowers are borne in clusters in early spring. Rarely in this country do we find this species of greater height than about 8 feet, but it is of bushy growth, though somewhat straggling in appearance. As early as the beginning of January this Witch Hazel may be found in bloom, the bare branches being studded here and there with the curious-shaped flowers, these having bright yellow, twisted petals and reddish calyces. H.j. Zuccarinianais a very desirable free-flowering variety, with pale yellow petals and a greenish-brown calyx.

H. VIRGINICA.--Virginian Witch Hazel. North America, 1736. This has smaller flowers than H.j. arborea, and they are plentifully produced in autumn or early winter. In this country it assumes the shape of an open bush of about 6 feet in height, but is usually of untidy appearance from the branches being irregularly disposed.

They all delight in cool, rather moist soil, and are of value for their early-flowering nature.

HEDYSARUM.

HEDYSARUM MULTIJUGUM.--South Mongolia. Hardly ten years have elapsed
since this pretty shrub was introduced into England, so that at present it is rather rare in our gardens. It is a decided acquisition, if only for the production of flowers at a time when these are scarce. Usually the flowering time is in August, but frequently in the first weeks of October the pretty flowers are still full of beauty. It is of bushy habit, from 4 feet to 5 feet high, with oblong leaflets, in number from twenty to thirty-five, which are Pea-green above and downy on the under sides. Flowers bright red, and produced in axillary racemes. It is perfectly hardy, and grows freely in porous decomposed leaf-soil.

HELIANTHEMUM.

HELIANTHEMUM HALIMIFOLIUM.--Spain, 1656. This species is of erect habit, 3 feet or 4 feet high, and with leaves reminding one of those of the Sea

Purslane. It is an evergreen, and has large bright yellow flowers, slightly spotted at the base of the petals.

H. LAEVIPES (syn Cistus laevipes).--South-western Europe. A dwarf shrub, with Heath-like leaves, and yellow flowers that are produced in great abundance.

H. LASIANTHUM (syns H. formosum and *Cistus formosus*).--Spain and Portugal, 1780. This is a beautiful species, but not hardy unless in the South and West. It has large, bright yellow flowers, with a deep reddish-purple blotch at the base of each petal.

H. LAVENDULAEFOLIUM has lavender-like leaves, with the under surface hoary, and yellow flowers. A native of the Mediterranean regions.

H. LIBONATES.--This species bears dark green Rosemary-like leaves, and yellow flowers that are produced very abundantly. South Europe.

H. PILOSUM.--South of France, 1831. This bears white flowers that are of good substance, and about an inch across.

H. POLIFOLIUM (syn H. pulverulentum).--Europe (Britain), and North Africa. This is a neat-growing shrub, of very dwarf growth, with hairy leaves and yellow flowers; and H. polifolium roseum, has pretty rosy-red flowers.

H. UMBELLATUM.--South Europe, 1731. A neat, small-growing species, with
white flowers and glossy-green leaves covered with a rusty-white tomentum beneath.

H. VULGARE.--Common Rock Rose. Europe (Britain), North Africa, and West Asia. A widely distributed native plant, of dwarf growth, with linear-oblong, hairy leaves, and usually yellow flowers. H. vulgare nummularium differs in having the leaves green and sub-orbicular, with yellow flowers. H. vulgare barbaturn is of erect habit, with silky, hairy, oval leaves. H. vulgare mutabile bears pale rose flowers, marked with yellow at the base. H. vulgare grandiflorum is remarkable for the large, bright yellow flowers, and is one of the most beautiful and worthy varieties. H. vulgare ovalifolium (syn H. serpyllifolium) bears yellow flowers and ovate leaves, with the margins revolute. H. vulgare hyssopifolium bears reddish flowers, but the colouring varies considerably, and saffron is not uncommon.

The Rockroses are very valuable plants, in that they will succeed on poor, gravelly banks where few other plants could eke out an existence. They cannot withstand stiff soil, nor that at all inclined to be damp, their favourite resorts being exposed, rocky ground, and dry, gravelly banks. Being readily increased from cuttings, which take root well under a hand glass or in a cool house, it is advisable, at least with the more tender forms, to have at hand a stock, so that blanks in the shrubbery may be filled up.

HIBISCUS.

HIBISCUS SYRIACUS (syn Althaea frutex).--Syrian Mallow. Syria, 1596. An old occupant of our gardens, and one that cannot be too freely cultivated. When favourably situated, it often reaches 6 feet in height, with three-lobed, neatly-toothed leaves, and with large, showy blossoms that are borne towards the end of summer. The typical species has purplish flowers, with a crimson spot at the base of each petal, but others, varying in colour from snow-white to purple and blue, are common in cultivation. H. syriacus coelestis bears bright blue flowers, while H. syriacus variegatus has beautifully variegated foliage. Of the double-flowered forms, there are several beautiful and worthy plants, the following list containing some of the best varieties of this popular shrub:--

H. syriacus albo-pleno.
" amaranthus.
" amplissima.
" ardens.
" caerulea plena.
" carnea plena.
" De la Veuve.
" elegantissimum.
" fastuosa.
" Lady Stanley.
" Leopoldii.
" lilacina plena.
" paeoniaeflora.
" puniceus plenus.
" rosea plena.
" rubra plena.
" spectabilis plena.
" violacea.

HIPPOPHAE.

HIPPOPHAE RHAMNOIDES.--Sea Buckthorn, or Sallow Thorn. Though generally considered as a sea-side shrub, the Sea Buckthorn is by no means exclusively so, thriving well, and attaining to large dimensions, in many inland situations. The flowers are not at all conspicuous, but this is amply compensated for by the beautiful silvery-like leaves and wealth of fruit borne by the shrub. In not a few instances, for fully a foot in length, the branches are smothered with crowded clusters of bright orange berries, and which render the shrub during November and December both distinct and effective. It does best in sandy soil, and is readily increased from suckers, which are usually plentifully produced by old plants. For sea-side planting it is one of our most valuable shrubs, succeeding, as it does, well down even to high water mark, and where the foliage is lashed with the salt spray.

HOLBOELLIA.

HOLBOELLIA LATIFOLIA (syn Stauntonia latifolia).--Himalayas, 1840. An evergreen climbing shrub that is more often found under glass than out of doors. In the South of England, however, it is quite hardy against a sunny wall. It grows 12 feet high, with shining green leathery leaves, and fragrant purplish-green flowers. H. latifolia angustifolia has decidedly narrower leaves than the species, but is in no other way different.

HYDRANGEA.

HYDRANGEA ARBORESCENS.--North America, 1736. This is a plant of large growth, but the flowers are greenish-white, and by no means conspicuous.

H. HORTENSIS (syn Hortensia opuloides).--China, 1790. This is an old-fashioned garden shrub that is only hardy in the south and west of these islands and in the vicinity of the sea. In some of the forms nearly all the flowers are sterile, the calyx-lobes being greatly expanded, and in others the outer flowers only are sterile. According to the nature of the soil the flowers vary much in colour, some being pure white, others pink, and others of varying shades of blue. There are some very beautiful and distinct varieties, such as H. hortensis japonica; H. hortensis Otaksa, with large panicles of sterile blue flowers; H. hortensis rosea-alba, with large rosy flowers; H. hortensis Thomas Hogg, a very free-flowering and welcome form; H. hortensis mandschurica, and H. hortensis stellata flore-pleno, with partially double flowers, are worthy of attention.

H. PANICULATA.--Japan, 1874. This is one of the most distinct species, in which the flower-heads are elongated, not flat, as in most other species, and from which the finest form in cultivation has been obtained. This is H. paniculata grandiflora, in which the flowers are sterile and pure white, forming large panicles often a foot in length. It is a magnificent variety, and, being perfectly hardy, should be extensively planted for ornament. The flowers are produced in late summer, but remain in good form for fully two months, dying off a rich reddish hue.

H. QUERCIFOLIA.--Oak-leaved Hydrangea. Florida, 1803. This species has neatly lobed leaves, and terminal panicles of pinky-white, but partially barren, flowers.

H. SCANDENS.--Climbing Hydrangea. Japan, 1879. This is not very hardy, but with the protection of a sunny wall it grows freely.

The Hydrangeas require a rich, loamy soil, and, unless in maritime districts, a warm and sheltered situation. They are readily propagated by means of cuttings.

HYMENANTHERA.

HYMENANTHERA CRASSIFOLIA.--A curious New Zealand shrub with rigid ashy-coloured branches, and small leathery leaves. The flowers are violet-like in colour, but by no means conspicuous. The small white berries which succeed the flowers are, in autumn, particularly attractive, and very ornamental. It is perfectly hardy and of free growth in light peaty earth.

HYPERICUM.

HYPERICUM ANDROSAEMUM.--Tutsan, or Sweet Amber. Europe (Britain). A pretty native species, growing about 2 feet high, with ovate leaves having glandular dots and terminal clustered cymes of yellow flowers.

H. AUREUM.--South Carolina and Georgia, 1882. This soon forms a neat and handsome plant. The flowers are unusually large, and remarkable for the tufts of golden-yellow stamens with which they are furnished.

H. CALYCINUM.--Aaron's Beard, or Rose of Sharon. South-east Europe. This is a well-known native species of shrubby growth, bearing large yellow flowers from 3 inches to 4 inches in diameter. It is a prostrate plant, with coriaceous glossy leaves with small pellucid dots, and of great value for planting in the shade.

H. ELATUM is a spreading species from North America (1762), growing to fully 4 feet in height, and bearing terminal corymbs of large, bright yellow flowers in July and August. Leaves rather large, oblong-ovate, and revolute. On account of its spreading rapidly from the root, this species requires to be planted where it will have plenty of room.

H. HIRCINUM.--Goat-scented St. John's Wort. Mediterranean region, 1640. A small-growing and slender species, with oblong-lanceolate leaves 2 inches long, and producing small yellow flowers in terminal heads. There is a smaller growing form known as H. hircinum minus. The plant emits a peculiar goat-like odour.

H. MOSERIANUM is a beautiful hybrid form with red anthers.

H. OBLONGIFOLIUM (syns H. Hookerianum and *H. nepalensis*).--Nepaul, 1823. An evergreen species, about 4 feet high, with oblong, pellucid, dotted leaves, and deep golden, somewhat waxy flowers at the end of summer.

H. PROLIFICUM.--North America, 1758. This is a much branched twiggy shrub, about 4 feet high, with small, linear-lanceolate leaves, thickly studded with pellucid dots. Flowers not very large, five-petalled, and of a pleasing bright yellow colour. The allied if not identical H. Kalmiana is worthy of being included in a selection of these plants.

H. URALUM.--Nepaul, 1823. A neat but fragile species that attains to about a yard in height. Leaves rather small, elliptic, almost stalkless, and perforated with transparent dots. Flowers small and of a bright golden yellow.

H. fasciculatum, H. pyrimidatum, and H. patulum are all worthy of attention, where a good representative collection is of importance. The Hypericums succeed best when planted in a rather sandy and not too dry loam, and they are readily increased either from divisions or by means of cuttings.

IDESIA.

IDESIA POLYCARPA (syns Flacourtica japonica and *Polycarpa Maximowiczii*).--A Japanese tree of small growth, and only introduced to this country in 1866. It is a handsome, hardy species, bearing large, bright-green leaves with conspicuous crimson footstalks, often 4 inches across, and of a glaucous tint on the under sides. The deliciously fragrant flowers are greenish-white or yellowish-green, and produced in graceful drooping racemes. In southern England it does well, and, being a tree of unusual beauty of both leaves and flowers, is well worthy of attention. Rich loam, not too stiff, will grow the Idesia well.

ILEX.

ILEX AQUIFOLIUM.--Common Holly. Europe (Britain) and West Asia. Though
the Hollies are not usually reckoned ornamental for the sake of their flowers, their berries are highly so. Some of them are nevertheless deliciously fragrant when in bloom. The leaves of this, our native species, in their typical form are oblong-ovate, wavy, and deeply spiny-toothed. The tree flowers in May and June, while the clusters of bright red berries ripen in autumn, persist all the winter, and sometimes even hang on tree till a second crop is matured, provided they are not devoured by birds during severe weather. The varieties are very numerous, and differ chiefly in the form and toothing of the leaves, which are variegated in many cases, their size and form, and in the colour of the berries in a few instances.

I. Aquifolium albo-marginata has ovate, nearly flat, spiny-serrate leaves, with a narrow silvery margin, and fruits freely. I. Aquifolium fructu albo has white berries; in I. Aquifolium fructu luteo they are yellow and very abundantly produced; and in I. Aquifolium fructu nigro they are black. I. Aquifolium handsworthensis has elliptic-oblong spiny leaves, with a creamy-white margin and marbled with gray. Grafted trees bear berries in great profusion from the time they are only a foot high, and are highly ornamental. I. Aquifolium Hodginsii has large, broadly oblong-ovate, slightly spiny leaves, and large crimson-red berries that ripen late in autumn. I. Aquifolium Hodginsii aurea is a sub-variety with a broad golden margin to the leaves, and the disc splashed with gray. Beautiful and distinct is I. Aquifolium Lawsoniana, with ovate, flat, almost spineless leaves, heavily and irregularly blotched with yellow in the centre. The berries are of a brilliant red. The variety differs from Milkmaid in having flat, nearly entire leaves. I. Aquifolium pendula has a wide, rounded, drooping head, but otherwise does not differ from the type. Many others bear berries, but the above are all very distinct forms.

I. OPACA.--American Holly. United States, 1744. The leaves of this species are oblong or oval, small, spiny-serrate, and of a dark opaque green. The berries, which ripen in autumn, are small, bright red, and very liable to be eaten by birds. In America this Holly is put to precisely the same purposes as the common Holly is in Europe. It is perfectly hardy here.

ILLICIUM.

ILLICIUM FLORIDANUM, from Florida (1771), is a beautiful but uncommon shrub, probably on account of its being tender and susceptible to injury by frost, unless in the warmer and more favoured parts of the country. The fragrant flowers are of a purplish-rose, while the foliage is neat and of a pleasing green.

I. ANISATUM (syn I. religiosum), from China and Japan (1842), is too tender for outdoor culture in this country.

INDIGOFERA.

INIDGOFERA GERARDIANA (syns I. floribunda and *I. Dosua*).--India, 1842. This forms a compact dwarf bush in the open, but is still better suited for covering a wall, the growth and floriferousness being then much increased. The foliage is neat and Pea-green, while the bright pink

Pea-like flowers are produced in long racemes. It is a pretty bush, and grows freely enough in any good garden soil, but very fine flowering specimens may be seen in light, sandy soil of a peaty nature. There is a white flowered variety named I. Gerardiana alba.

ITEA.

ITEA VIRGINICA.--North America, 1744. This is a neat, deciduous shrub of 3 feet or 4 feet in height. The ovate-lanceolate leaves are of a light greyish-green, and the small white flowers are produced in dense racemes or spikes. Planted in a somewhat shady place, and in rather cool, damp soil, this little shrub does well and flowers profusely.

JAMESIA.

JAMESIA AMERICANA.--Rocky Mountains and Colorado, 1865. Amongst early
spring-flowering shrubs this pretty but neglected plant is one of the best, of perfect hardihood, for it stands the vigour of our winters with impunity, and of dense thick growth; it is suitable for using in a variety of ways, as well as for purely ornamental purposes. The leaves are oval and neatly dentated, and the flowers individually of large size, pure white, and produced in terminal bunches. Cool soil and a shady situation would seem to suit the plant admirably, but for screen purposes in the rock garden or border it is invaluable on account of the strong and dense twigs.

JASMINUM.

JASMINUM FRUTICANS.--South Europe, 1570. An evergreen species, well adapted, from its rather stiff and upright growth, for planting alone. It has trifoliolate leaves and showy yellow flowers.

J. HUMILE.--India, 1656. A hardy species of dwarf growth, and bearing beautiful golden flowers produced in summer.

J. NUDIFLORUM.--Naked Jasmine. China, 1844. A showy and well-known species, from China, with numerous, usually solitary yellow flowers, ternate leaves, and flexible branches. The variety J. nudiflorum aureo-variegatum has golden-variegated leaves.

J. OFFICINALE.--Northern India to Persia, 1548. The white-flowered Jasmine of our gardens is a very beautiful and desirable clambering shrub, either for wall covering, for planting by tree stumps, rooteries, or rockeries, or for screening and draping the pergola or garden latticework. From its great hardihood, vigour of growth, and beauty of flowers, it is certainly one of the most deservedly popular of wall shrubs. The branches are deep green, angular, and flexible, the leaves pinnate, and the flowers pure-white and sweetly-scented. The variety J. officinale affine has flowers that are individually larger than those of the species; J. officinale aurea has badly variegated leaves; J. officinale grandiflorum and J. officinale grandiflorum majus, are also desirable kinds.

J. PUBIGERUM GLABRUM (syn J. Wallichianum), from North-west India, is not well-known, being tender in most parts of the country.

J. REVOLUTUM.--India, 1812. This has persistent dark, glossy-green leaves, and fragrant, bright yellow flowers, produced in large, terminal clusters. From India, but perfectly hardy as a wall plant, and for which purpose, with its bright evergreen leaves, it is well suited.

As regards soil, the Jasmines are very accommodating, and are propagated by layers or cuttings.

KADSURA.

KADSURA JAPONICA.--Japan, 1846. This is a small-growing shrub, with lanceolate and pointed leaves, that are remotely dentated. The flowers are not very showy, being of a yellowish-white colour and about an inch across. They are produced both terminal and axillary, and in fair abundance. The scarlet fruits are arranged in clusters, and when fully ripe are both showy and interesting. Generally speaking this shrub suffers from severe frost, but as only the branch tips are injured, it shoots freely from the stock. It produces its flowers in the autumn. There is a variety with variegated leaves.

KALMIA.

KALMIA ANGUSTIFOLIA.--Sheep Laurel. Canada, 1736. This is at once distinguished from K. latifolia by its much smaller and narrower leaves and smaller flowers, which latter are, however, of brighter tint and more plentifully produced. It rarely exceeds 2 feet in height. Of this there are two very distinct forms, that named K. angustifolia pumila, being of neat and dense small growth; and K. angustifolia rubra, in which the flowers are of an unusually deep red.

K. GLAUCA.--Canada and Sitcha, 1767. This, which has lilac-purple flowers, produced in early spring, is not a very desirable species, being rather straggling of growth and with few flowers.

K. HIRSUTA.--Hairy-leaved Kalmia. South-east Virginia to Florida, 1786. This is at once distinguished by the rather rough and hairy foliage and few rosy-tinted flowers. It is of dwarf, neat growth.

K. LATIFOLIA.--Calico Bush, or Mountain Laurel. Alleghanies, Canada, and Western Florida, 1734. A favourite shrub in every garden where the conditions of soil will allow of its being successfully cultivated. In peaty soil, or light, friable loam and leaf soil, it forms a dense, round-headed bush, often 8 feet in height, and nearly as much through, with pleasing green leaves, and dense clusters of beautiful pink, wax-like flowers. The flowering period commences in May, and usually extends to the end of July. This is a choice shrub of great hardihood, and one of the handsomest flowering in cultivation. There is a still more beautiful form named K. latifolia major splendens, and one with small Myrtle-like foliage named K. latifolia myrtifolia.

The members of this handsome family are, as a rule, partial to cool, damp soil, peat of a light, sandy nature being preferred. They thrive well where Azaleas and Rhododendrons will succeed. In bold masses they have a fine effect, but a well developed standard specimen of the commonly cultivated species is highly ornamental.

KERRIA.

KERRIA JAPONICA (syn Corchorus japonicus).--Japan, 1700. A Japanese shrub, the double-flowered variety of which, K. japonica flore-pleno, is one of our commonest wall plants. The orange-yellow flowers, produced in great rosettes, are highly ornamental, and have earned for the shrub a well-known name. It succeeds well almost anywhere, and, though usually seen as a wall plant, is perfectly hardy, and forms a neat shrub for the open border. There is a form in which the leaves are variegated, and known under the name of K. japonica variegata.

KOELREUTERIA.

KOELREUTERIA PANICULATA.--Northern China, 1763. Whether for its foliage or flowers, this small-growing tree is worthy of a place. Though of rather irregular growth, the beautiful foliage and large panicles of yellowish flowers, which stand well above the leaves, make the shrub (for it does not in this country attain to tree height), one of particular interest, and a valuable aid in ornamental planting. In a sheltered corner, and planted in rich soil, it grows and flowers freely.

LABURNUM.

LABURNUM ADAMI (syn Cytisus Adami).--A graft hybrid form between the common Laburnum and Cytisus purpureus, the result being flowers of the Laburnum, the true Cytisus purpureus, and the graft hybrid between the two. It was raised by Jean Louis Adam in 1825. It is a curious and distinct tree, worthy of culture if only for the production of three distinct kinds of flowers on the same plant.

L. ALPINUM (syn Cytisus alpinus).--Scotch Laburnum. Europe, 1596. This very closely resembles the common Laburnum, but it is of larger growth, and flowers later in the season. The flowers, too, though in longer racemes, are usually less plentifully produced. It grows 30 feet high. There is a weeping form, L. alpinum pendulum, and another with fragrant flowers, named L. alpinum fragrans, as also a third, with very long racemes of flowers, named L. alpinum Alschingeri.

L. CARAMANICUM.--Asia Minor, 1879. A bushy shrub of vigorous habit, with trifoliolate and petiolate leaves of a pale green colour, thick and tough, and brightly polished on the upper surface. Flowers bright yellow, the calyx being helmet-shaped and rusty-red. It is a beautiful but uncommon shrub, and succeeds very well in chalky or calcareous soil.

Flowers in July.

L. VULGARE (syn Cytisus Laburnum).--Common Laburnum. Southern France to Hungary, 1596. This is one of our commonest garden and park trees, and at the same time one of the most beautiful and floriferous. The large, pendulous racemes of bright yellow flowers are, when at their best in May, surpassed neither in quantity nor beauty by those of any other hardy tree. There are several varieties of this Laburnum--a few good, but many worthless, at least from a garden point of view. L. vulgare Parkesii is a seedling form, bearing large racemes of deep-coloured flowers, often 14 inches long; L. vulgare Watereri was raised in the Knap Hill Nursery, Surrey, and is one of the most distinct and beautiful of the many forms into which the Laburnum has been sub-divided. The flower racemes are very long and richly coloured. L. vulgare quercifolium and L. vulgare sessilifolium are fairly well described by their names; L. vulgare fragans differs only in having sweetly-scented flowers; L. vulgare involutum has curiously-curled leaves; while L. vulgare aureum, where it does well, is a beautiful and distinct form.

LARDIZABALA.

LARDIZABALA BITERNATA.--Chili, 1848. Requires wall protection, there being few situations in which it will succeed when planted in the open. It is a tall, climbing shrub, with dark green persistent leaves, and bearing purplish flowers in drooping racemes in mid-winter. Planted in rather dry soil, at the base of a sunny wall, this shrub forms a by no means unattractive covering, the twice ternate, glossy leaves being fresh and beautiful the winter through.

LAPAGERIA.

LAPAGERIA ROSEA.--Chili, 1847. This is, unfortunately, not hardy, unless in favoured maritime districts, but in such situations it has stood unharmed for many years, and attained to goodly proportions. It is a beautiful climber, with deep-green leaves, and large, fleshy, campanulate flowers of a deep rose colour. There is a white-flowered form called L. alba, introduced from Chili in 1854. Planted on an east aspect wall, and in roughly broken up peat and gritty sand, it succeeds well.

LAVANDULA.

LAVANDULA VERA (syn L. Spica).--Common Lavender. South Europe, 1568. A well-known and useful plant, but of no particular value for ornamental purposes. It is of shrubby growth, with narrow-lanceolate, hoary leaves, and terminal spikes of blue flowers.

LAVATERA.

LAVATERA ARBOREA.--Tree Mallow. Coasts of Europe, (Britain). A stout-growing shrub reaching in favourable situations a height of fully 6 feet, with broadly orbicular leaves placed on long stalks. The flowers are plentiful and showy, of a pale purplish-red colour, and collected into clusters. It is a seaside shrub succeeding best in sheltered maritime recesses, and when in full flower is one of the most ornamental of our native plants. There is also a beautiful variegated garden form, L. a. variegata.

LEDUM.

LEDUM LATIFOLIUM (syn L. groenlandicum).--Wild Rosemary, or Labrador Tea. This is a small shrub, reaching to about 3 feet in height, indigenous to swampy ground in Canada, Greenland, and over a large area of the colder parts of America. Leaves oval or oblong, and plentifully produced all over the plant. Flowers pure white, or slightly tinted with pink, produced in terminal corymbs, and usually at their best in April. A perfectly hardy, neat-growing, and abundantly-flowered shrub, but one that, somehow, has gone greatly out of favour in this country. This plant has been sub-divided into several varieties, that are, perhaps, distinct enough to render them worthy of attention. They are L. latifolium globosum, with white flowers, borne in globose heads, on the short, twiggy, and dark-foliaged branches. L. latifolium angustifolia has narrower leaves than those of the species, while L. latifolium intermedium is of neat growth and bears pretty, showy flowers.

L. PALUSTRE.--Marsh Ledum. This is a common European species, growing from 2 feet to 3 feet high, with much smaller leaves than the former, and small pinky-white flowers produced in summer. It is an interesting and pretty plant. The Ledums succeed best in cool, damp, peaty soil.

LEIOPHYLLUM.

LEIOPHYLLUM BUXIFOLIUM (syns L. thymifolia, Ammyrsine buxifolia and Ledum buxifolium).--Sand Myrtle. New Jersey and Virginia, 1736. This is a dwarf, compact shrub from New Jersey, with box-like leaves, and bunches of small white flowers in early summer. For using as a rock plant, and in sandy peat, it is an excellent subject, and should find a place in every collection.

LESPEDEZA.

LESPEDEZA BICOLOR (syn Desmodium penduliflorum).--North China and Japan. A little-known but beautiful small-growing shrub, of slender, elegant growth, and reaching, under favourable culture, a height of about 6 feet. The leaves are trifoliolate, small, and neat, and the abundant racemes of individually small, Pea-shaped flowers are of the richest and showiest reddish-purple. Being only semi-hardy will account for the scarcity of this beautiful Japanese shrub, but having stood uninjured in all but the coldest parts of these islands should induce lovers of flowering shrubs to give it a fair chance.

LEUCOTHOE.

LEUCOTHOE AXILLARIS (syn Andromeda axillaris).--North America, 1765. This is of small growth, from 2 feet to 3 feet high, with oval-pointed leaves and white flowers in short racemes produced in May and June. It is not a very satisfactory species for cultivation in this country.

L. CATESBAEI (syns Andromeda Catesbaei and *A. axillaris*).--North America. This has white flowers with an unpleasant odour like that of Chestnut blossoms, but is worthy of cultivation, and succeeds best in cool sandy peat or friable yellow loam.

L. DAVISIAE, from California (1853), is a very handsome evergreen shrub, of small and neat growth, and will be found an acquisition where compact shrubs are in demand. The leaves are small, of a deep green colour, and remain throughout the year. Flowers produced in great abundance at the branch tips, usually in dense clusters, and individually small and pure white.

L. RECURVA (syn Andromeda recurva).--North America. A very distinct plant on account of the branch tips being almost of a scarlet tint, and thus affording a striking contrast to the grayish-green of the older bark. The flowers are pinky-white and produced in curving racemes and abundantly over the shrub. Like other members of the family it delights to grow in cool sandy peat.

LEYCESTERIA.

LEYCESTERIA FORMOSA, from Nepaul (1824), is an erect-growing, deciduous shrub, with green, hollow stems, and large ovate, pointed leaves of a very deep green colour. The flowers are small, and white or purplish, and produced in long, pendulous, bracteate racemes from the axils of the upper leaves. It is one of the most distinct and interesting of hardy shrubs, the deep olive-green of both stem and leaves, and abundantly-produced and curiously-shaped racemes, rendering it a conspicuous object wherever planted. Perfectly hardy, and of free, almost rampant growth in any but the stiffest soils. Cuttings root freely and grow rapidly.

LIGUSTRUM.

LIGUSTRUM IBOTA (syn L. amurense).--Japan, 1861. A compact growing species, about 3 feet in height, with small spikes of pure white flowers produced freely during the summer months.

L. JAPONICUM (syns L. glabrum, L. Kellennanni, L. Sieboldii and *L. syringaeflorum*).--Japan Privet. This is a dwarf-growing species rarely exceeding 4 feet in height, with broad, smooth, glossy-green leaves, and large compound racemes of flowers. There are several varieties, including L. japonicum microphyllum, with smaller leaves than the parent; and one with tricoloured foliage and named L. japonicum variegatum.

L. LUCIDUM (syns L. magnoliaefolium and **L. strictum**).--Shining-leaved Privet, or Woa Tree. China, 1794. A pretty evergreen species, with oval leaves, and terminal, thyrsoid panicles of white flowers. It is an old inhabitant of our gardens, and forms a somewhat erect, twiggy bush, of fully 10 feet in height. Of this there are two varieties, one with larger bunches of flowers, and named L. lucidum floribundum, and another with variegated leaves, L. lucidum variegatum. L. lucidum coriaceum (Leathery-leaved Privet) is a distinct variety, with thick, leathery-green leaves, and dense habit of growth.

L. OVALIFOLIUM (syn L. californicum).--Oval-leaved Privet. Japan, 1877. This is a commonly-cultivated species, with semi-evergreen leaves, and spikes of yellowish-white flowers. It is a good hedge plant, and succeeds well as a town shrub. There are several variegated forms, of which L. ovalifolium variegatum (Japan, 1865) and L. ovalifolium aureum are the best.

L. QUIHOI.--China, 1868. This is a much valued species, as it does not flower until most of its relations have finished. Most of the Privets flower at mid-summer, but this species is often only at its best by the last week of October and beginning of November. It forms a straggling freely-branched shrub, of fully 6 feet in height and nearly as much through, with dark shining-green oblong leaves, and loose terminal panicles of pure white, powerfully-scented flowers. It flourishes, like most of the Privets, on poor soil, and is a little-known species that note should be made of during the planting season.

L. SINENSE (syns L. villosum and **L. Ibota villosum**).--Chinese Privet. China, 1858. This is a tall deciduous shrub, with oblong and tomentose leaves, and flowers in loose, terminal panicles and produced freely in August. L. sinense nanum is one of the prettiest forms in cultivation. It is almost evergreen, with a horizontal mode of growth, and dense spikes of crearny-white flowers, so thickly produced as almost to hide the foliage from view. It is a most distinct and desirable variety.

L. VULGARE.--Common Privet. Although one of our commonest shrubs, this Privet can hardly be passed unnoticed, for the spikes of creamy-white flowers, that are deliciously scented, are both handsome and effective. Of the common Privet there are several distinct and highly ornamental forms, such as L. vulgare variegatum, L. vulgare pendulum, having curiously-creeping branches, and the better-known and valuable L. vulgare sempervirens (syn L. italicum), the Italian Privet.

LINNAEA.

LINNAEA BOREALIS.--Twin Flower. A small and elegant, much-creeping evergreen shrub, with small, ovate crenate leaves, and pairs of very fragrant, pink flowers. Two conditions are necessary for its cultivation--a half-shaded aspect where bottom moisture is always present, and a deep, rich, friable loam. A native of Scotland and England, flowering in July.

LIPPIA.

LIPPIA CITRIODORA (syns Aloysia citriodora and *Verbena triphylla*).--Lemon-scented Verbena. Chili, 1794. With its slender branches and pale green, pleasantly-scented, linear leaves, this little plant is a general favourite that needs no description. The flowers are not very ornamental, being white or lilac, and produced in small, terminal panicles. A native of Chili, it is not very hardy, but grown against a sunny wall, and afforded the protection of a mat in winter, with a couple of shovelfuls of cinders heaped around the stem, it passes through the most severe weather with little or no injury, save, in some instances, the branch tips being killed back. Propagated readily from cuttings placed in a cool frame or under a hand-light.

LIRIODENDRON.

LIRIODENDRON TULIPIFERA.--Tulip Tree. North America, 1688. One of the noblest hardy exotic trees in cultivation. The large, four-lobed, truncate leaves, of a soft and pleasing green, are highly ornamental, and are alone sufficient to establish the identity of the tree. Flowers large, yellow, and sweet-scented, and usually freely produced when the tree has attained to a height of between 20 feet and 30 feet. When we consider the undoubted hardihood of the tree and indifference to soil, its noble aspect, handsome foliage that is so distinct from that of any other tree, and showy flowers, we feel justified in placing it in the very first rank of ornamental trees. L. tulipifera integrifolia has entire leaves, which render it distinct from the type; L. tulipifera fastigiata, or pyramidalis, is of erect growth; L. tulipifera aurea, with golden foliage; and L. tulipifera crispa, with the leaves curiously undulated--a peculiarity which seems constant, but is more curious than beautiful. Few soils come amiss to the Tulip Tree, it thriving well in that of very opposite descriptions--loam, almost pure gravel, and alluvial deposit.

LONICERA.

LONICERA CAPRIFOLIUM.--Europe. This species resembles L. Periclymenum, but is readily distinguished by the sessile flower-heads, and fawny-orange flowers.

L. FLEXUOSA (syn L. brachypoda).--Japan, 1806. This is a pretty species, and one of the most useful of the climbing section. By its slender, twining, purplish stems, it may at once be distinguished, as also by the deep green, purplish-tinted leaves, and sweetly-scented flowers of various shades of yellow and purple. A native of China, and perfectly hardy as a wall plant. L. flexuosa aureo-reticulata is a worthy variety, in which the leaves are beautifully netted or variegated with yellow.

L. FRAGRANTISSIMA.--China, 1845. This species is often confounded with L. Standishii, but differs in at least one respect, that the former is strictly a climber, while the latter is of bushy growth. The leaves, too, of L. Standishii are hairy, which is not the case with the other species. It is a very desirable species, with white fragrant flowers, produced during the winter season.

L. PERICLYMENUM.--Honeysuckle, or Woodbine. An indigenous climbing shrub, with long, lithe, and twisted cable-like branches, and bearing heads of sweetly-scented, reddish-yellow flowers. This is a favourite wild plant, and in the profusion and fragrance of its flowers it is surpassed by none of the exotic species. There are several distinct nursery forms of this plant, including those known as L. Periclymenum Late Dutch, L. Periclymenum Early Cream, and L. Periclymenum odoratissimum; as also one with variegated foliage.

L. SEMPERVIRENS.--Scarlet Trumpet Honeysuckle. A North American evergreen species (1656), with scarlet, almost inodorous flowers, produced freely during the summer. For wall covering it is one of the most useful of the family. The variety L. sempervirens minor is worthy of attention.

L. STANDISHII, a Chinese species (1860), has deliciously fragrant while flowers, with a slight purplish tint, and is well worthy of attention, it soon forming a wall covering of great beauty.

L. TATARICA.---Tartarian Honeysuckle. Tartary, 1752. This is a very variable species, in so far at least as the colour of flowers is concerned, and has given rise to several handsome varieties. The typical plant has rosy flowers, but the variety L. tatarica albiflora has pure white flowers; and another, L. tatarica rubriflora has freely produced purplish-red flowers.

L. XYLOSTEUM (syn Xylosteum dumetorum).--Fly Honeysuckle. Europe (England) to the Caucasus. The small, creamy-white flowers of this plant are not particularly showy, but the scarlet berries are more conspicuous in September and October. The gray bark of the branches has also a distinct effect in winter when grown in contrast to the red-barked species of Cornus, Viburnum, and yellow-barked Osier. It is one of the oldest occupants of British shrubberies. L. Xylosteum leucocarpum has white berries; those of L. Xylosteum melanocarpum are black; and in L. Xylosteum xanthocarpum they are yellow.

The Honeysuckles are all of the readiest culture, and succeed well in very poor soils, and in that of opposite qualities. Propagated from cuttings or by layering.

LOROPETALON.

LOROPETALON CHINENSE.--Khasia Mountains and China, 1880. This is a pretty and interesting shrub belonging to the more familiar Witch Hazel family. Flowers clustered in small heads, the calyx pale green, and the long linear petals almost pure white. Being quite hardy, and interesting as well as ornamental, should insure this Chinese shrub a place in every good collection.

LYCIUM.

LYCIUM BARBARUM.--Box Thorn, or Tea Tree. North Asia, 1696. A pretty lax, trailing shrub, with long, slender, flexible twigs, small linear-lanceolate leaves, and rather sparsely-produced lilac or violet flowers. Planted against a wall, or beside a stout-growing, open-habited shrub, where the peculiarly lithe branches can find support, this plant does best. Probably nowhere is the Box Thorn so much at home as in seaside places, it then attaining to sometimes 12 feet in height, and bearing freely its showy flowers during summer, and the bright scarlet or orange berries in winter.

L. EUROPAEUM.--European Box Thorn. South Europe, 1730. This is a spiny, rambling shrub, that may often be seen clambering over some cottage porch, or used as a fence or wall plant in many parts of England. It often grows nearly 20 feet long, and is then a plant of great beauty, with linear-spathulate leaves of the freshest green, and pretty little pink or reddish flowers. For quickly covering steep, dry banks and mounds where few other plants could exist this European Box Thorn is invaluable. Either species will grow in very poor, dry soil, and is readily propagated by means of cuttings.

LYONIA.

LYONIA PANICULATA (syns L. ligustrina, Andromeda globulifera, A. pilifera, and *Menziesia globularis*).--North America, 1806. This species grows about a yard high, with clustered, ovate leaves, and pretty, pinky, drooping flowers.

MACLURA.

MACLURA AURANTIACA.--Osage Orange, or Bow-wood. North America, 1818. This is a wide-spreading tree with deciduous foliage, and armed with spines along the branches. The leaves are three inches long, ovate and pointed, and of a bright shining green. Flowers rather inconspicuous, being green with a light tinge of yellow, and succeeded by fruit bearing a resemblance when ripe to the Seville orange. It is hardy, and grows freely in rather sandy or gravelly soil.

MAGNOLIA.

MAGNOLIA ACUMINATA.--Cucumber Tree. North America, 1736. This is a large and handsome species, of often as much as 50 feet in height, and with a head that is bushy in proportion. The leaves are 6 inches long, ovate and pointed, and of a refreshing shade of green. Flowers greenish-yellow, sweetly scented, and produced abundantly all over the tree. They are succeeded by small, roughish fruit, resembling an infant cucumber, but they usually fall off before becoming ripe.

M. CAMPBELII.--Sikkim, 1868. This is a magnificent Indian species, but, unfortunately, it is not hardy except in the favoured English and Irish localities. The leaves are large, and silky on the undersides, while the flowers are crimson and white, and equally as large as those of the better-known M. grandiflora.

M. CONSPICUA (syn M. Yulan).--Yulan. China, 1789. A large-growing shrub, with Pea-green, deciduous foliage, and large, pure white flowers that oft get damaged by the spring frosts. M. conspicua Soulangeana is a supposed hybrid between M. conspicua and M. obovata. Whatever may be the origin of this Magnolia, it is certainly a handsome and showy plant of very vigorous growth, producing freely its white, purple-tinted flowers, and which last for a long time in perfection. There are several other varieties, including M. conspicua Soulangeana nigra, with dark purplish flowers; M. conspicua Alexandrina, M. conspicua Soulangeana speciosa, and M. conspicua Norbertii.

M. CORDATA, a native of the Southern Alleghanies (1801), is still rare in collections. It is a small-growing, deciduous species, with yellow flowers, that are neither scented nor showy.

M. FRASERI (syn M. auriculata).--Long-leaved Cucumber Tree. North America, 1786. This species has distinctly auriculated leaves and large, yellowish-white, fragrant flowers.

M. GLAUCA.--Laurel Magnolia. North America, 1688. This is one of the commonest species in our gardens, and at the same time one of the hardiest. It is of shrub size, with Laurel-like leaves, and sweetly-scented, small, pure white flowers, produced about the end of June.

M. GRANDIFLORA.--North America, 1737. One of the handsomest species, with very large, glossy, evergreen leaves, and deliciously odoriferous, creamy-white flowers, that are often fully 6 inches across. It is usually seen as a wall plant, and the slight protection thus afforded is almost a necessity in so far as the development of the foliage and flowers is concerned. M. grandiflora exoniensis (Exmouth Magnolia) is a very handsome form.

M. LENNEI.--This is a garden hybrid between M. conspicua and M. obovata discolor, and has flowers as large as a goose's egg, of a rosy-purple colour, and produced profusely.

M. MACROPHYLLA.--North America, 1800. This species has very large leaves and flowers, larger, perhaps, than those of any other species. They are very showy, being white with a purple centre. It attains a height of 30 feet.

M. OBOVATA DISCOLOR (syn M. purpurea).--Japan, 1790. This is a small-growing, deciduous shrub, with large, dark green leaves, and Tulip-shaped flowers, that are purple on the outside and almost white within.

M. PARVIFLORA, from Japan, with creamy-white, fragrant flowers, that are globular in shape, is a very distinct and attractive species, but cannot generally be relied upon as hardy.

M. STELLATA (syn M. Halleana).--Japan, 1878. A neat, small-growing, Japanese species, of bushy habit, and quite hardy in this country. The small, white, fragrant flowers are produced abundantly, even on young plants, and as early as April. One of the most desirable and handsome of the small-growing species. M. stellata (pink variety) received an Award of Merit at the meeting of the Royal Horticultural Society on March 28, 1893. This bids fair to be really a good thing, and may best be described as a pink-flowered form of the now well-known and popular species.

M. UMBRELLA (syn M. tripetala).--Umbrella Tree. North America, 1752. A noble species, with large, deep green leaves, that are often 16 inches long. It is quite hardy around London, and produces its large, white, fragrant flowers in succession during May and June. The fruit is large and showy, and of a deep purplish-red colour.

MEDICAGO.

MEDICAGO ARBOREA.--South Europe, 1596. This species grows to the height of 6 feet or 8 feet, and produces its Pea-shaped flowers from June onwards. The leaves are broadly oval and serrated at the tips, but they vary in this respect. It is not hardy unless in warm, sheltered corners of southern England and Ireland, although it stood unharmed for many years at Kew. It succeeds best, and is less apt to receive injury, when planted in rather dry and warm soil.

MENISPERMUM.

MENISPERMUM CANADENSE.--Moonseed. North America, 1691. This shrub is principally remarkable for the large, reniform, peltate leaves, which are of value for covering pergolas, bowers and walls. The flowers are of no great account, being rather inconspicuous and paniculate. It is hardy in most places, and is worthy of culture for its graceful habit and handsome foliage.

MICROGLOSSA.

MICROGLOSSA ALBESCENS (syn Aster albescens and *A. cabulicus*).--Himalayas, 1842. This member of the Compositae family is a much-branched shrub, with grayish lanceolate foliage, and clusters of flowers about 6 inches in diameter, and of a bluish or mauve colour. It is a native of Nepaul, and, with the protection of a wall, perfectly hardy around London.

MITCHELLA.

MITCHELLA REPENS.--Partridge Berry. North America, 1761. A low-growing, creeping plant, having oval, persistent leaves, white flowers, and brilliant scarlet fruit. It is a neat little bog plant, resembling Fuchsia procumbens in habit, and with bunches of the brightest

Cotoneaster-like fruit. For rock gardening, or planting on the margins of beds in light, peaty soil, this is one of the handsomest and most beautiful of hardy creeping shrubs.

MITRARIA.

MITRARIA COCCINEA.--Scarlet Mitre Pod. Chiloe, 1848. This is only hardy in the South of England and Ireland, and even there it requires wall protection. It is a pretty little shrub, with long, slender shoots, which, during the early part of the summer, are studded with the bright red, drooping blossoms, which are urn-shaped, and often nearly 2 inches long. It delights in damp, lumpy, peat.

MYRICA.

MYRICA ASPLENIFOLIA (syn Comptonia asplenifolia).--Sweet Fern. North America, 1714. A North American plant of somewhat straggling growth, growing to about 4 feet high, and with linear, pinnatified, sweet-smelling leaves. The flowers are of no decorative value, being small and inconspicuous, but for the fragrant leaves alone the shrub will always be prized. It grows well in peaty soil, is very hardy, and may be increased by means of offsets. This shrub is nearly allied to our native Myrica or Sweet Gale.

M. CALIFORNICA.--Californian Wax Myrtle. California, 1848. In this we have a valuable evergreen shrub that is hardy beyond a doubt, and that will thrive in the very poorest classes of soils. In appearance it somewhat resembles our native plant, but is preferable to it on account of the deep green, persistent leaves. The leaves are about 3 inches long, narrow, and produced in tufts along the branches. Unlike our native species, the Californian Wax Myrtle has no pleasant aroma to the leaves.

M. CERIFERA.--Common Candle-berry Myrtle. Canada, 1699. This is a neat little shrub, usually about 4 feet high, with oblong-lanceolate leaves, and inconspicuous catkins.

M. GALE.--Sweet Gale or Bog Myrtle. This has inconspicuous flowers, and is included here on account of the deliciously fragrant foliage, and which makes it a favourite with cultivators generally. It is a native shrub, growing from 3 feet to 4 feet high, with deciduous, linear-lanceolate leaves, and clustered catkins appearing before the leaves. A moor or bog plant, and of great value for planting by the pond or lake side, or along with the so-called American plants, for the aroma given off by the foliage.

The Myricas are all worthy of cultivation, although the flowers are inconspicuous--their neat and in most cases fragrant foliage, and adaptability to poor soil or swampy hollows, being extra recommendations.

MYRTUS.

MYRTUS COMMUNIS.--Common Myrtle. South Europe, 1597. A well-known shrub,
which, unless in very favoured spots and by the sea-side, cannot survive our winters. Where it does well, and then only as a wall plant, this and its varieties are charming shrubs with neat foliage and an abundance of showy flowers. The double-flowered varieties are very handsome, but they are more suitable for glass culture than planting in the open.

M. LUMA (syn Eugenia apiculata and *E. Luma*).--Chili. Though sometimes seen growing out of doors, this is not to be recommended for general planting, it being best suited for greenhouse culture.

M. UGNI (syn Eugenia Ugni).--Valdivia, 1845. A small-growing, Myrtle-like shrub, that is only hardy in favoured parts of the country. It is of branching habit, with small, wiry stems, oval, coriacious leaves, and pretty pinky flowers. The edible fruit is highly ornamental, being of a pleasing ruddy tinge tinted with white. This dwarf-growing shrub wants the protection of a wall, and when so situated in warm seaside parts of the country soon forms a bush of neat and pleasing appearance.

NEILLIA.

NEILLIA OPULIFOLIA (syn Spiraea opulifolia).--Nine Bark. North America, 1690. A hardy shrub, nearly allied to Spiraea. It produces a profusion of umbel-like corymbs of pretty white flowers, that are succeeded by curious swollen membraneous purplish fruit. N. opulifolia aurea is worthy of culture, it being of free growth and distinct from the parent plant.

N. THYRSIFLORA, Nepaul, 1850, would seem to be quite as hardy as N. opulifolia, and is of more evergreen habit. The leaves are doubly serrated and three lobed, and cordate-ovate. Flowers white in spicate, thyrsoid racemes, and produced rather sparsely.

NESAEA.

NESAEA SALICIFOLIA (syn Heimia salicifolia).--Mexico, 1821. This can only be styled as half hardy, but with wall protection it forms a pretty bush often fully a yard in height. The leaves resemble those of some species of Willow, being long and narrow, while the showy yellow flowers are freely produced in August and September. It thrives best when planted in light, dry soil, and in a sheltered position.

NEVIUSA.

NEVIUSA ALABAMENSIS.--Alabama Snow Wreath. Alabama, 1879. This is a rare American shrub, with leaves reminding one of those of the Nine Bark, Neillia opulifolia, and the flowers, which are freely produced along the full length of the shoots, are white or yellowish-green, with prominent stamens of a tufted brush-like character. It is usually treated as a green-house plant, but may be seen growing and flowering freely in the open ground at Kew.

NUTTALLIA.

NUTTALLIA CERASIFORMIS.--Osoberry. California, 1848. This shrub is of great value on account of the flowers being produced in the early weeks of the year, and when flowers are few and far between. It grows from 6 feet to 10 feet high, with a thick, twiggy head, and drooping racemes of white flowers borne thickly all over the plant. Few soils come amiss to this neglected shrub, it growing and flowering freely even on poor gravelly clay, and where only a limited number of shrubs could succeed.

OLEARIA.

OLEARIA HAASTII.--New Zealand, 1872. This Composite shrub is only hardy in the milder parts of England and Ireland. It is of stiff, dwarf growth, rarely growing more than 4 feet high, but of neat and compact habit. Flowering as it does in late summer it is rendered of special value, the Daisy-like white blossoms being produced in large and flat clusters at the branch tips. The leaves are neat and of leathery texture, and being evergreen lend an additional charm to the shrub.

O. MACRODONTA (syn O. dentata), from New Zealand, 1886, is tolerably hardy, and may be seen in good form both at Kew and in the South of Ireland. The large Holly-like leaves are of a peculiar silvery-green tint above, and almost white on the under sides. Flowers white, and produced in dense heads in June and July.

O. Forsterii and O. Gunniana (syn Eurybia Gunniana) are nearly hardy species, the latter, from New Zealand, bearing a profusion of white Daisy-like flowers on dense, twiggy branches.

ONONIS.

ONONIS ARVENSIS.--Restharrow. A native undershrub of very variable size, according to the position in which it is found growing. It creeps along the ground, the shoots sending out roots as they proceed, and is usually found on dry sandy banks. The flowers when at their best are very ornamental, being bright pink, and with the standard streaked with a deeper shade. They are abundantly produced, and render the plant very conspicuous during the summer and autumn months. When planted on an old
wall, and allowed to roam at will, the Restharrow is, perhaps, seen to best advantage.

OSMANTHUS.

OSMANTHUS AQUIFOLIUM ILLICIFOLIUS.--Holly-leaved Osmanthus. Japan. This is a handsome evergreen shrub, with Holly-like leaves, and not very conspicuous greenish-white flowers. It is a very desirable shrub, of which there are varieties named O.A. ilicifolius argenteo-variegatus, O.A. ilicifolius aureo-variegatus, and O.A. ilicifolius nanus, the names of which will be sufficient to define their characters.

O.A. ILICIFOLIUS MYRTIFOLIUS.--Myrtle-leaved Osmanthus. A very distinct and beautiful shrub, with unarmed leaves. It is of dwarf, compact growth, with small, sharply-pointed leaves, and inconspicuous flowers. For the front line of a shrubbery this is an invaluable shrub, its pretty leaves and neat twiggy habit making it a favourite with planters. The variety rotundifolius is seldom seen in cultivation, but being distinct in foliage from any of the others is to be recommended. They grow freely in any good garden soil, but all the better if a little peat is added at the time of planting.

OSTRYA.

OSTRYA CARPINIFOLIA (syn O. vulgaris).--Common Hop Hornbeam. South Europe, 1724. A much-branched, round-headed tree, with cordate-ovate, acuminate leaves. Both this and the following species, by reason of the resemblance between their female catkins and those of the Hop, and between their leaves and those of the Hornbeam, have acquired the very descriptive name of Hop Hornbeam. This is a large-growing tree, specimens in various parts of the country ranging in height from 50 feet to 60 feet.

O. VIRGINICA.--Virginian Hop Hornbeam. Eastern United States, 1692. Resembles the latter, but is of smaller growth, rarely exceeding 40 feet in height. They grow fairly well in almost any class of soil, and on account of the long and showy catkins are well worthy of cultivation.

OXYDENDRUM.

OXYDENDRUM ARBOREUM (syn Andromeda arborea).--Sorrel-tree. Eastern United States, 1752. Unfortunately this species is not often found under cultivation, being unsuitable generally for our climate. In some instances, however, it has done well, a specimen in the Knap Hill Nursery, Surrey, being 30 feet high, and with a dense rounded head. The flowers are very beautiful, being of a waxy white, and produced abundantly. It wants a free rich soil, and not too exposed site.

OZOTHAMNUS.

OZOTHAMNUS ROSMARINIFOLIUS.--Australia, 1827. A pretty little Australian
Composite, forming a dense, twiggy shrub, with narrow, Rosemary-like leaves, and small, whitish, Aster-like flowers which resemble those of its near relative, the Olearia, and are produced so thickly that the plant looks like a sheet of white when the blooms are fully developed. It flowers in June and July. In most parts of the country it will require protection, but can be classed as fairly hardy. Cuttings root freely if placed in sandy soil in a cool frame.

PAEONIA.

PAEONIA MOUTAN.--Moutan Paeony, or Chinese Tree Paeony. China and Japan, 1789. A beautiful shrubby species introduced from China about one hundred years ago. The first of the kind introduced to England had single flowers, and the plant is figured in Andrews' ***Botanists' Repository*** (tab. 463) under the name of P. papaveracea. The flowers are white with a dark red centre. In the ***Botanical Magazine*** (tab. 2175), the same plant is figured under the name of P. Moutan var. papaveracea. This is perfectly hardy in our gardens, and is the parent of many beautiful and distinct varieties, including double and single white, pink, crimson, purple, and striped.

PALIURUS.

PALIURUS ACULEATUS (syn P. australis).--Christ's Thorn, or Garden Thorn. Mediterranean region, 1596. A densely-branched, spiny shrub, with small leaves, and not very showy, yellowish-green flowers. It grows and flowers freely enough in light, peaty earth, but is not very hardy, the tips of the branches being usually killed back should the winter be at all severe.

PARROTIA.

PARROTIA PERSICA.--Persia, 1848. Well known for the lovely autumnal tints displayed by the foliage when dying off. But for the flowers, too, it is well worthy of culture, the crimson-tipped stamens of the male flowers being singularly beautiful and uncommon. In February it is no unusual sight to see on well-established plants whole branches that are profusely furnished with these showy flowers. For planting in a warm corner of a rather dry border it seems to be well suited; but it is perfectly hardy and free of growth when suited with soil and site. It is as yet rare in cultivation, but is sure, when better known and more widely disseminated, to become a general favourite with lovers of hardy shrubs.

PASSIFLORA.

PASSIFLORA CAERULEA.--Passion Flower. Brazil and Peru, 1699. Though not perfectly hardy, yet this handsome climbing plant, if cut down to the ground, usually shoots up freely again in the spring. The flowers, which are produced very freely, but particularly in maritime districts, vary from white to blue, and the prettily-fringed corona and centre of the flower render the whole peculiarly interesting and beautiful. P. caerulea Constance Elliott has greenish-white flowers; and P. caerulea Colvillei has white sepals and a blue fringe. The latter is of more robust growth, and more floriferous than the species.

PAULOWNIA.

PAULOWNIA IMPERIALIS.--Japan, 1840. This is a handsome, fast-growing tree, and one that is particularly valuable for its ample foliage, and distinct and showy flowers. Though perfectly hardy, in other respects it is unfortunate that the season at which the Paulownia flowers is so early that, unless the conditions are unusually favourable, the flower buds get destroyed by the frost. The tree grows to fully 40 feet high in this country, and is a grandly decorative object in its foliage alone, and for which, should the flowers never be produced, it is well worthy of cultivation. They are ovate-cordate, thickly covered with a grayish woolly tomentum, and often measure, but particularly in young and healthy trees, as much as 10 inches in length. The Foxglove-like flowers are purplish-violet and spotted, and borne in terminal panicles. They are sweetly-scented. When favourably situated, and in cool, sandy loam or peaty earth, the growth of the tree is very rapid, and when a tree has been cut over, the shoots sent out often exceed 6 feet in length in one season, and nearly 2 inches in diameter. There are many fine old trees throughout the country, and which testify to the general hardihood of the Paulownia.

PERIPLOCA.

PERIPLOCA GRAECA.--Poison Vine. South Eastern Europe, and Orient, 1597. A tall, climbing shrub, with small, ovate-lanceolate leaves, and clusters of curious purplish-brown, green-tipped flowers produced in summer. The long, incurved appendages, in the shape of a crown, and placed so as to protect the style and anthers, render the flowers of peculiar interest. Though often used as a greenhouse plant, it is perfectly hardy, and makes a neat, deciduous wall or arch covering, thriving to perfection in rich soil that is well-drained. It is readily propagated from cuttings.

PERNETTYA.

PERNETTYA MUCRONATA (syn Arbutus mucronata).--Prickly Heath. Magellan, 1828. This is a dwarf-growing, wiry shrub, with narrow, stiff leaves, and bears an abundance of white, bell-shaped flowers. It is a capital wind screen, and may be used to advantage on the exposed side of rockwork or flower beds, or as an ornamental shrub by the pond or lake side. The small dark-green leaves, the tiny white flowers, and great abundance of deep purple berries in winter, are all points that are in favour of the shrub for extended cultivation. The pretty, pinky shoots, too, help to make the plant attractive even in mid-winter. Propagation by layers or seed is readily brought about. To grow this shrub to perfection, peaty soil or decayed vegetable matter will be found most suitable. There is a narrow-leaved form named P. mucronata angustifolia, and another on which the name of P. mucronata speciosa has been bestowed.

There are many beautiful-berried forms of the Pernettya, but as their flowers are small can hardly be included in our list.

PHILADELPHUS.

PHILADELPHUS CORONARIUS.--Mock Orange, or Syringa. South Europe, 1596. A well-known and valuable garden shrub, of from 6 feet to 10 feet high, with ovate and serrulated leaves, and pretty racemes of white or yellowish-white, fragrant flowers. P. coronarius aureo-variegatus is one of the numerous forms of this shrub, having brightly-tinted, golden foliage, but the flowers are in no way superior to those of the parent. It is, if only for the foliage, an extremely pretty and distinct variety. P. coronarius argenteo-variegatus has silvery-tinted leaves; P. coronarius flore-pleno, full double flowers; and P. coronarius Keteleeri flore-pleno is the best double-flowered form in cultivation.

P. GORDONIANUS, an American species (1839), is a well-known and beautiful shrub, in which the flowers are usually double the size of those of the common species, and which are not produced till July, while those of P. coronarius appear in early May.

P. GRANDIFLORUS (syns P. floribundus, P. latifolius and *P. speciosus*).--Southern United States, 1811. This has rotundate, irregularly-toothed leaves, and large white, sweetly-scented flowers produced in clusters. This forms a stout bush 10 feet high, and as much through. There are two varieties, P. grandiflorus laxus, and P. grandiflorus speciosissimus, both distinct and pretty kinds.

P. HIRSUTUS.--North America, 1820. Another handsome, small-flowered species, of dwarf growth, and having hairy leaves.

P. INODOROUS, also from North America (1738), differs little in size and shape of flowers from P. grandiflorus, but the flowers are without scent. The leaves, too, are quite glabrous and obscurely toothed.

P. LEMOINEI BOULE D'ARGENT is a cross, raised in 1888, from P. Lemoinei and the double-flowered form of P. coronarius. The flowers are double white and with the pleasant, but not heavy, scent of P. microphyllus. P. Lemoinei Gerbe de Neige bears pleasantly-scented flowers that are as large as those of the well-known P. speciosissimus. There is an erect form of P. Lemoinei named erectus that is also worthy of note.

P. LEWISI, from North America, is hardly sufficiently distinct from some of the others to warrant special notice.

P. MICROPHYLLUS, from New Mexico (1883), is of low growth, and remarkable for its slender branches, small, Myrtle-like leaves, and abundance of small, white flowers. It is a decidedly pretty shrub, but is not so hardy as the others.

P. SATZUMI (syn P. chinensis).--Japan, 1851. A slender-growing species, with long and narrow leaves, and large, white flowers.

P. TRIFLORUS and P. MEXICANUS are other species that might be worthy of including in a representative collection of these plants.

This is a valuable genus of shrubs, all being remarkable for the abundance of white, and usually sweet-scented, flowers which they produce. They require no special treatment, few soils, if at all free and rich, coming amiss to them; while even as shrubs for shady situations they are not to be despised. Propagation is effected by means of cuttings, which root freely if placed in sandy soil.

PHILLYREA.

P. ANGUSTIFOLIA (narrow-leaved Phillyrea), P. ilicifolia (Holly-leaved Phillyrea), P. salicifolia (Willow-leaved Phillyrea), P. buxifolia (Box-leaved Phillyrea), and P. ligustrifolia (Privet-leaved Phillyrea), are all more or less valuable species, and their names indicate their peculiarities of leafage. P. angustifolia rosmarinifolia (syn P. neapolitana) is a somewhat rare shrub, but one that is well worthy of culture, if only for its neat habit and tiny little Rosemary-like leaves. It is from Italy, and known under the synonym of *P. rosmarinifolia*.

P. LATIFOLIA (syn P. obliqua).--Broad-leaved Phillyrea. South Europe, 1597. This is a compact-growing and exceedingly ornamental shrub, with bright and shining, ovate-serrulated leaves. For its handsome, evergreen foliage and compact habit of growth it is, perhaps, most to be valued, for the small flowers are at their best both dull and inconspicuous. Not very hardy unless in the sea-coast garden.

P. MEDIA (syns P. ligustrifolia and *P. oleaefolia*).--South Europe, 1597. This is another interesting species, but not at all common in cultivation.

P. VILMORINIANA (syns P. laurifolia and *P. decora*).--Asia Minor, 1885, This is a grand addition to these valuable shrubs, of which it is decidedly the best from an ornamental point of view. It is of compact growth, with large, Laurel-like leaves, which are of a pleasing shade of green, and fully 4 inches long. They are of stout, leathery texture, and plentifully produced. That this shrub is perfectly hardy is now a well-established fact.

The Phillyreas succeed well in light, warm, but not too dry soil, and they do all the better if a warm and sheltered position is assigned to them. Being unusually bright of foliage, they are of great service in planting for shrubbery embellishment, and which they light up in a very conspicuous manner during the dull winter months. They get shabby and meagre foliaged if exposed to cold winds.

PHLOMIS.

PHLOMIS FRUTICOSA.--Jerusalem Sage. Mediterranean region, 1596. This is a neat-growing shrubby plant, with ovate acute leaves, that are covered with a yellowish down. From the axils of the upper leaves the whorls of yellow flowers are freely produced during the summer months. It is valued for its neat growth, and as growing on dry soils where few other plants could eke out an existence.

PHOTINIA.

PHOTINIA JAPONICA (syn Eriobotrya japonica).--Loquat, Japan Medlar, or Japan Quince. Japan, 1787. This is chiefly remarkable for its handsome foliage, the leaves being oblong of shape and downy on the under sides. The white flowers are of no great beauty, but being produced at the beginning of winter, and when flowers are scarce, are all the more welcome. It requires protection in all but the warmer parts of these islands.

P. ARBUTIFOLIA (syns Crataegus arbutifolia and ***Mespilus arbutifolia***).--Arbutus-leaved Photinia, or Californian May-bush. California, 1796. This is a very distinct shrub, with leaves resembling those of the Strawberry Tree (Arbutus), the flowers in an elongated panicle, and bright red bark on the young wood.

P. BENTHAMIANA is only worthy of culture for its neat habit and freedom of growth when suitably placed.

P. SERRULATA (syn Crataegus glabra).--Chinese Hawthorn. Japan and China, 1804. This has Laurel-like leaves, 4 inches or 5 inches long, and, especially when young, of a beautiful rosy-chocolate colour, and clustered at the branch-tips. Flowers small, white, and produced in flat corymbs. An invaluable seaside shrub.

They all grow well either in light, rich loam, or in sandy, peaty earth, and are usually propagated by grafting.

PHYLODOCE.

PHYLODOCE TAXIFOLIA (syns P. caerulea and *Menziesia caerulea*).--An almost extinct native species, having crowded linear leaves, and lilac-blue flowers. It is only of value for rock gardening.

PIERIS.

PIERIS FLORIBUNDA (syns Andromeda floribunda and *Leucothoe floribunda*).--United States, 1812. Few perfectly hardy shrubs are more beautiful than this, with its pure white Lily-of-the-Valley like flowers, borne in dense racemes and small, neat, dark green leaves. To cultivate this handsome shrub in a satisfactory way, fairly rich loam or peat, and a situation sheltered from cold and cutting winds, are necessities.

P. JAPONICA (syn Andromeda japonica).--Japan, 1882. A hardy, well-known shrub, that was first brought specially under notice in "The Garden," and of which a coloured plate and description were given. It is thickly furnished with neat and small deep-green, leathery leaves, and pretty, waxy white flowers, pendulous at the branch tips. Planted in free, sandy peat, it thrives vigorously, and soon forms a neat specimen of nearly a yard in height. It is a very desirable hardy species, and one that can be confidently recommended for ornamental planting. There is a variegated variety, P. japonica elegantissima, with leaves clearly edged with creamy-white, and flushed with pink. Amongst variegated, small-growing shrubs it is a gem.

P. MARIANA (syn Andromeda Mariana ovalis).--North America, 1736. A neat shrub of about 3 feet in height, with oval leaves, and pretty white flowers in pendent clusters.

P. OVALIFOLIA (syn Andromeda ovalifolia).--Nepaul, 1825. A fine, tall-growing species, with oval-pointed, leathery leaves placed on long footstalks. Flowers in lengthened, drooping, one-sided racemes, and white or pale flesh-coloured. Being perfectly hardy, and attaining to as much as 20 feet in height, it is a desirable species for the lawn or shrubbery.

PIPTANTHUS.

PIPTANTHUS NEPALENSIS (syn Baptisia nepalensis).--Evergreen Laburnum. Temperate Himalaya, 1821. A handsome, half-hardy shrub, of often fully 10 feet high, with trifoliolate, evergreen leaves, and terminal racemes of large yellow flowers. In the south and west of England and Ireland it does well, and only receives injury during very severe winters. Planted either as a single specimen, or in clumps of three or five, the evergreen Laburnum has a pleasing effect, whether with its bright, glossy-green leaves, or abundance of showy flowers. It is of somewhat erect growth, with stout branches and plenty of shoots. Propagated from seed, which it ripens abundantly in this country.

PITTOSPORUM.

PITTOSPORUM TOBIRA.--Japan, 1804. This forms a neat, evergreen shrub, with deep green, leathery leaves, and clusters of white, fragrant flowers, each about an inch in diameter. It is hardy in the more favoured parts of the south and west of England, where it makes a reliable seaside shrub.

P. UNDULATUM, from Australia (1789), is also hardy against a wall, but cannot be depended upon generally. It is a neat shrub, with wavy leaves, that are rendered conspicuous by the dark midribs. They grow well in any good garden soil.

PLAGIANTHUS.

PLAGIANTHUS LYALLI, a native of New Zealand (1871), and a member of the Mallow family, is a free-flowering and beautiful shrub, but one that cannot be recommended for general planting in this country. At Kew it does well and flowers freely on an east wall. The flowers are snow-white, with golden-yellow anthers, and produced on the ends of the last season's branchlets during June and July. The flower-stalks, being fully 2 inches long, give to the flowers a very graceful appearance. In this country the leaves are frequently retained till spring.

P. LAMPENI.--Van Dieman's Land, 1833. This is about equally hardy with the former, and produces a great abundance of sweetly-scented flowers.

P. PULCHELLUS (syn Sida pulchella).--Australia and Tasmania. Another half-hardy species, which bears, even in a young state, an abundance of rather small, whitish flowers.

POLYGALA.

POLYGALA CHAMAEBUXUS.--Bastard Box. A neat little shrubby plant, with small ovate, coriaceous leaves, and fragrant yellow and cream flowers. P. chamaebuxus purpureus differs in bearing rich reddish-purple flowers, and is one of the most showy and beautiful of rock plants. They are natives of Europe (1658), and grow best in vegetable mould.

POTENTILLA.

POTENTILLA FRUTICOSA.--Northern Hemisphere (Britain). An indigenous shrub that grows about a yard high, with pinnate leaves and golden flowers. It is a most persistent blooming plant, as often for four months, beginning in June, the flowers are produced freely in succession. It delights to grow in a strong soil, and, being of low, sturdy growth, does well for the outer line of the shrubbery.

PRUNUS.

PRUNUS AMYGDALUS (syn Amygdalus communis).--Common Almond. Barbary, 1548. Whether by a suburban roadside, or even in the heart of the crowded city, the Almond seems quite at home, and is at once one of the loveliest and most welcome of early spring-flowering trees. The flowers are rather small for the family, pale pink, and produced in great quantity before the leaves. There are several distinct forms of the Almond, differing mainly in the colour of the flowers, one being pink, another red, while a third has double flowers. P. Amygdalus macrocarpa (Large-fruited Almond) is by far the handsomest variety in cultivation, the flowers being large, often 3 inches in diameter, and white tinged with pink, particularly at the base of the petals. The flowers, too, are produced earlier than those of any other Almond, while the tree is of stout growth and readily suited with both soil and site.

P. AMYGDALUS DULCIS (syn A. dulcis), Sweet Almond, of which there are three distinct varieties, P.A. dulcis purpurea, P.A. dulcis macrocarpa, and P.A. dulcis pendula, should be included in every collection of these handsome flowering plants.

P. AVIUM JULIANA (syn Cerasus Juliana).--St. Julian's Cherry. South Europe. This bears large flowers of a most beautiful and delicate blush tint. P. Avium multiplex is a double form of the Wild Cherry, or Gean, with smaller leaves than the type.

P. BOISSIERII (syn Amygdalus Boissierii).--Asia Minor, 1879. This is a bushy shrub, with almost erect, long, and slender branches, and furnished with leaves an inch long, elliptic, and thick of texture. Flowers pale flesh-coloured, and produced abundantly. It is a very ornamental and distinct plant, and is sure, when better known, to attract a considerable amount of attention.

P. CERASIFERA (syn P. Myrobalana).--Cherry, or Myrobalan Plum. Native Country unknown. A medium-sized tree, with an abundance of small white flowers, which are particularly attractive if they escape the early spring frosts. It is of stout, branching habit, with a well-rounded head, and has of late years attracted a good deal of notice as a hedge plant. P. cerasifera Pissardii, the purple-leaved Cherry plum, is a remarkable and handsome variety, in which the leaves are deep purple, thus rendering the plant one of the most distinct and ornamental-foliaged of the family. It produces its white, blush-tinted flowers in May. It was received by M.A. Chatenay, of Sceau, from M. Pissard, director of the garden of His Majesty the Shah of Persia. When it flowered it was figured in the ***Revue Horticole***, 1881, p. 190.

P. CERASUS (syn Cerasus vulgaris).--Common Cherry. A favourite medium-sized tree, and one that lends itself readily to cultivation. As an ornamental park tree this Cherry, though common, must not be despised, for during summer, when laden with its pure white flowers, or again in autumn when myriads of the black, shining fruits hang in clusters from its branches, it will be readily admitted that few trees have a more beautiful or conspicuous appearance, P. Cerasus flore-pleno (double-flowered Cherry) is a distinct and desirable variety. P. Cerasus multiplex is a very showy double form, more ornamental than P. Avium muliplex, and also known under the names of *Cerasus ranunculiflora* and C. Caproniana multiplex. P. Cerasus semperflorens (syn Cerasus semperflorens), the All Saints, Ever Flowering, or Weeping, Cherry, is another valuable variety, of low growth, and with gracefully drooping branches, particularly when the tree is old. It is a very desirable lawn tree, and flowers at intervals during the summer.

P. CHAMAECERASUS (syn Cerasus Chamaecerasus).--Ground Cherry. Europe, 1597. This is a dwarf, slender-branched, and gracefully pendent shrub, of free growth, undoubted hardihood, and well worthy of extended cultivation. The variety C. Chamaecerasus variegata has the leaves suffused with greenish lemon. There is also a creeping form named P. Chamaecerasus pendula.

P. DAVIDIANA.--AbbE David's Almond. China. This is the tree to which, under the name of Amygdalus Davidiana alba, a First-class Certificate was awarded in 1892 by the Royal Horticultural Society. The typical species is a native of China, from whence it was introduced several years ago, but it is still far from common. It is the earliest of the Almonds to unfold its white flowers, for in mild winters some of them expand before the end of January; but March, about the first week, it is at its best. It is of more slender growth than the common Almond, and the flowers, which are individually smaller, are borne in great profusion along the shoots of the preceding year, so that a specimen, when in full flower, is quite one mass of bloom. There is a rosy-tinted form known as Amygdalus Davidiana rubra.

P. DIVARICATA, from the Caucasus (1822), is useful on account of the pure white flowers being produced early in the year, and before the leaves. It has a graceful, easy habit of growth, and inclined to spread, and makes a neat lawn or park specimen.

P. DOMESTICA, Common Garden Plum, and P. domestica insititia, Bullace Plum, are both very ornamental-flowering species, and some of the varieties are even more desirable than the parent plants.

P. ILLICIFOLIA (syn Cerasus ilicifolius).--Holly-leaved Cherry. California. A distinct evergreen species, with thick leathery leaves, and erect racemes of small white flowers. A native of dry hilly ground along the coast from San Francisco to San Diego. Hardy in most situations, but requiring light warm soil and a dry situation.

P. LAUNESIANA (syn Cerasus Launesiana).--Japan, 1870. This is a valuable addition to the already long list of ornamental-flowering Cherries. It flowers in the early spring, when the tree is literally enshrouded in rose-coloured flowers, and which produce a very striking effect. The tree is quite hardy, flowers well even in a young state, and will grow in any soil that suits our common wild species.

P. LAUROCERASUS (syn Cerasus Laurocerasus).--Common, or Cherry Laurel. Levant, 1629. Although a well-known garden and park shrub, of which a description is unnecessary, the common or Cherry Laurel, when in full flower, must be ranked amongst our more ornamental shrubs. There are several varieties all worthy of culture for the sake of their evergreen leaves and showy flower spikes. P. Laurocerasus rotundifolia has leaves that are broader in proportion to their length than those of the common species; P. Laurocerasus caucasica is of sturdy growth, with deep green leaves, and a compact habit of growth; P. Laurocerasus colchica is the freest-flowering Laurel in cultivation, with horizontally arranged branches and pale green leaves; P. Laurocerasus latifolia, a rather tender shrub, with bold handsome foliage; and P. Laurocerasus parvifolia, of low growth, but never very satisfactory in appearance. Three other less common forms might also be mentioned. P. Laurocerasus angustifolia, with narrow leaves; P. Laurocerasus camelliaefolia, with thick leathery foliage; and P. Laurocerasus intermedia, halfway between P. Laurocerasus angustifolia and the common Laurel.

P. LUSITANICA (syn Cerasus lusitanica).--Portugal Laurel. Portugal, 1648. A well-known shrub or small growing tree, and one of the most valuable of all our hardy evergreens. It is of neat and compact growth, with a good supply of bright green shining foliage, and bears long spikes of pleasing creamy white perfumed flowers. P. lusitanica myrtifolia (Myrtle-leaved Portugal Laurel) differs from the species in the smaller, longer, and narrower leaves, which are more thickly arranged, and in its more decided upright habit. P. lusitanica variegata is hardly sufficiently constant or distinct to warrant recommendation. P. lusitanica azorica, from the Azores, is of more robust growth than the common plant, with larger and richer green leaves, and the bark of the younger branches is of a very decided reddish tinge.

P. MAHALEB (syn Cerasus Mahaleb).--The Mahaleb, or Perfumed Cherry. South Europe, 1714. This and its variegated variety P. Mahaleb variegata are very free-flowering shrubs, and of neat growth. The variegated variety is well worthy of attention, having a clear silvery variegation, chiefly confined to the leaf margin, but in a less degree to the whole of the foliage, and imparting to it a bright, glaucous tint that is highly ornamental. There is a partially weeping form named P. Mahaleb pendula.

P. MARITIMA.--Beach or Sand Plum. North America, 1800. A prostrate, spreading shrub, that is of value for planting in poor sandy soil, and along the sea coast. The flowers are small, but plentifully produced.

P. NANA (syns Amygdalus nana and *A. Besseriana*).--Dwarf Almond. From Tartary, 1683. This is of dwarf, twiggy growth, rarely more than 3 feet high, and bearing an abundance of rose-coloured flowers in early

February. From its neat, small growth, and rich profusion of flowers, this dwarf Almond may be reckoned as a most useful and desirable shrub. Suckers are freely produced in any light free soil.

P. PADUS (syn Cerasus Padus).--Bird Cherry or Hagberry. An indigenous species, with oblong, doubly-serrated leaves, and terminal or axillary racemes of pure-white flowers. It is a handsome and distinct small-growing tree, and bears exposure at high altitudes in a commendable manner.

P. PANICULATA FLORE-PLENO (syns Cerasus serrulata flore-pleno and *C. Sieboldii*).--China, 1822. This is one of the most desirable of the small-growing and double-flowered Cherries. It is of neat growth, with short, stout branches that are sparsely furnished with twigs, and smooth, obovate, pointed leaves, bristly serrated on the margins. Flowers double and white at first, but afterwards tinged with pink, freely produced and of good, lasting substance. P. paniculata Watereri is a handsome variety that most probably may be linked to the species.

P. PENNSYLVANIA.--American Wild Red Cherry. North America, 1773. This is an old-fashioned garden tree, and one of the choicest, producing in May a great abundance of its tiny white flowers.

P. PERSICA FLORE-PLENO (syns Amygdalus Persica flore-pleno and Persica vulgaris), double-flowering Peach, is likewise well worthy of culture, there being white, rose, and crimson-flowering forms.

P. PUDDUM (syns P. Pseudo-cerasus and *Cerasus Pseudo-cerasus*).--Bastard Cherry. China, 1891. There are very few more ornamental trees in cultivation in this country than the double-flowering Cherry. It makes a charming small-growing tree, is of free growth and perfectly hardy, and one of, if not the most, floriferous of the tribe. The flowers are individually large, pinky or purplish-white, and produced with the leaves in April.

P. SINENSIS.--China, 1869. A Chinese Plum of somewhat slender growth, and with the branches wreathed in small, white flowers. It is often seen as a pot plant, but it is one of the hardiest of its family. P. sinensis flore-pleno is a double white form, and the most ornamental for pot work. There is also a variety with rose-coloured flowers.

P. SPINOSA.--Sloe, or Blackthorn. An indigenous, spiny shrub, with tiny white flowers; and P. spinosa flore-pleno has small, rosette-like flowers that are both showy and effective.

P. TOMENTOSA.--Japan, 1872. This is one of the most desirable of hardy shrubs, with large, white, flesh-tinted flowers produced in the first weeks of March, and in such quantities as almost to hide the branches from view. It forms a well-rounded, dense bush of 5 feet or 6 feet high.

P. TRILOBA (syns P. virgata, Amygdalopsis Lindleyi and **Prunopsis Lindleyi**).--China, 1857. This is a very handsome early-flowering shrub, that is at once recognised by the generally three-lobed leaves. It is one of the first to flower, the blossoms being produced in March and April, and sometimes even earlier when the plant is grown against a sunny, sheltered wall. The semi-double flowers are large and of good substance, and of a rosy-white tint, but deep rose in the bud state. There is a nursery form of this plant with white flowers, named P. triloba alba. It is quite hardy, bears pruning well, and grows quickly, soon covering a large space of a wall or warm, sunny bank. As an ornamental flowering lawn shrub it has few equals, the blossoms remaining good for fully a fortnight.

P. VIRGINIANA (syn Cerasus virginiana) and P. SEROTINA (North American Bird Cherries) are worthy species, with long clusters of flowers resembling those of our native Bird Cherry. They are large-growing species, and, particularly the latter, are finding favour with cultivators in this country on account of their bold and ornamental appearance.

PTELEA.

PTELEA TRIFOLIATA.--Hop Tree, or Swamp Dogwood. North America, 1704. A small-growing tree, with trifoliolate, yellowish-green leaves placed on long footstalks, and inconspicuous greenish flowers. The leaves, when bruised, emit an odour resembling Hops. P. trifoliata variegata is one of the handsomest of golden-leaved trees, and is well worthy of extensive planting. It is preferable in leaf colouring to the golden Elder. Perfectly hardy.

PUNICA.

PUNICA GRANATUM.--Pomegranate. For planting against a southern-facing wall this pretty shrub is well suited, but it is not sufficiently hardy for the colder parts of the country. Frequently in the more favoured parts of the country it reaches a height of 14 feet, with a branch-spread of nearly as much, and is then, when in full flower, an object of general admiration and of the greatest beauty. The flowers are of a rich, bright scarlet colour, and well set off by the glossy, dark green leaves. P. Granatum rubra flore-pleno is a decidedly ornamental shrub, in which the flowers are of a bright scarlet, and perfectly double. They grow satisfactorily in light, but rich soil.

PYRUS.

PYRUS ARIA.--White Beam Tree. Europe (Britain). A shrub or small-growing tree, with lobed leaves, covered thickly on the under sides with a close, flocculent down. The flowers are small and white, and produced in loose corymbs. It is a handsome small tree, especially when the leaves are ruffled by the wind and the under sides revealed to view. The red or scarlet fruit is showy and beautiful.

P. AUCUPARIA.--Mountain Ash, or Rowan Tree. Too well-known to need description, but one of our handsomest small-growing trees, and whether for the sake of its dense corymbs of small white flowers or large bunches of scarlet fruit it is always welcomed and admired. P. Aucuparia pendula has the branches inclined to be pendulous; and P. Aucuparia fructo-luteo differs from the normal plant in having yellowish instead of scarlet fruit.

P. AMERICANA (syn Sorbus americana).--American Mountain Ash. This species, a native of the mountains of Pennsylvania and Virginia (1782), is much like our Rowan Tree in general appearance, but the bunches of berries are larger, and of a brighter red colour.

P. ANGUSTIFOLIA.--North America, 1750. A double-flowered crab is offered under this name, of vigorous growth, bearing delicate pink, rose-like flowers that are deliciously fragrant, and borne contemporaneously with the leaves. The merits claimed for the shrub are perfect hardihood, great beauty of blossom and leaf, delicious fragrance, and adaptability to various soils. The single-flowered form extends over large areas in the Atlantic States of North America. They are very desirable, small-growing trees, and are described by Professor Sargent as being not surpassed in beauty by any of the small trees of North America.

P. BACCATA.--Siberian Crab. Siberia and Dahuria, 1784. This is one of the most variable species in cultivation, and from which innumerable forms have been developed, that differ either in habit, foliage, flowers, or fruit. The deciduous calyx would seem to be the only reliable distinguishing character. It is a widely-distributed species, being found in North China and Japan, Siberia and the Himalayas, and has from time immemorial been cultivated by the Chinese and Japanese, so that it is not at all surprising that numbers of forms have been developed.

P. CORONARIA.--Sweet Scented Crab. North America, 1724. This is a handsome species, with ovate, irregularly-toothed leaves, and pink and white fragrant flowers. The flowers are individually large and corymbose, and are succeeded by small green fruit.

P. DOMESTICA (syn Sorbus domestica).--True Service. Britain. This resembles the Mountain Ash somewhat, but the flowers are panicled, and the berries fewer, larger, and pear-shaped. The flowers are conspicuous enough to render the tree of value in ornamental planting.

P. FLORIBUNDA (syns P. Malus floribunda and *Malus microcarpa floribunda*).--China and Japan, 1818. The Japanese Crabs are wonderfully floriferous, the branches being in most instances wreathed with flowers that are individually not very large, and rarely exceeding an inch in diameter when fully expanded. Generally in the bud state the flowers are of a deep crimson, but this disappears as they become perfectly developed, and when a less striking tint of pinky-white is assumed. From the St. Petersburgh gardens many very ornamental Crabs have been sent out, these differing considerably in colour of bark, habit, and tint of flowers. They have all been referred to the above species. P. floribunda is a worthy form, and one of the most brilliant of spring-flowering trees. The long, slender shoots are thickly covered for almost their entire length with flowers that are rich crimson in the bud state, but paler when fully opened. There are numerous, very distinct varieties, such as P. floribunda atrosanguinea, with deep red flowers; P. floribunda Elise Rathe, of pendulous habit; P. floribunda John Downie, very beautiful in fruit; P. floribunda pendula, a semi-weeping variety; P. floribunda praecox, early-flowering; P. floribunda mitis, of small size; P. floribunda Halleana or Parkmanii, probably the most beautiful of all the forms; and P. floribunda Fairy Apple and P. floribunda Transcendant Crab, of interest on account of their showy fruit. P. floribunda Toringo (Toringo Crab) is a Japanese tree of small growth, with sharply cut, usually three-lobed, pubescent leaves, and small flowers. Fruit small, with deciduous calyx lobes.

P. GERMANICA (syn Mespilus germanica).--Common Medlar. Europe (Britain), Asia Minor, Persia. Early records show that the Medlar was cultivated for its fruit as early as 1596. Some varieties are still grown for that purpose, and in that state the tree is not devoid of ornament. The large, white flowers are produced singly, but have a fine effect in their setting of long, lanceolate, finely-serrate leaves during May.

P. JAPONICA (syn Cydonia japonica).--Japanese Quince. Japan, 1815. This is one of the commonest of our garden shrubs, and one that is peculiarly well suited for our climate, whether planted as a standard or as a wall plant. The flowers are brilliant crimson, and plentifully produced towards the end of winter and before the leaves. Besides the species there are several very fine varieties, including P. japonica albo cincta, P. japonica atropurpurea, P. japonica coccinea, P. japonica flore-pleno, P. japonica nivalis, a charming species, with snowy-white flowers; P. japonica rosea, of a delicate rose-pink; and P. japonica princeps. P. japonica cardinalis is one of the best of the numerous forms of this beautiful shrub. The flowers are of large size, of full rounded form, and of a deep cardinal-rose colour. They are produced in great quantity along the branches. A well-grown specimen is in April a brilliant picture of vivid colour, and the shrub is sooner or later destined to a chief place amongst our ornamental flowering shrubs. P. japonica Maulei (syn Cydonia Maulei), from Japan (1874), is a rare shrub as yet, small of growth, and with every twig festooned with the brightest of orange-scarlet flowers. It is quite hardy, and succeeds well under treatment that will suit the common species.

P. PRUNIFOLIA.--Siberia, 1758. Whether in flower or fruit this beautiful species is sure to attract attention. It is a tree of 25 feet in height, with nearly rotundate, glabrous leaves on long footstalks, and pretty pinky-white flowers. The fruit is very ornamental, being, when fully ripe, of a deep and glowing scarlet, but there are forms with yellow, and green, as also striped fruit.

P. RIVULARIS.--River-side Wild Service Tree. North-west America, 1836. A native of North America, with terminal clusters of white flowers, succeeded by sub-globose red or yellow fruit, is an attractive and handsome species. The fruit is eaten by the Indians of the North-west, and the wood, which is very hard and susceptible of a fine polish, is largely used in the making of wedges. It is a rare species in this country.

P. SINICA (syn P. sinensis of Lindley).--Chinese Pear Tree. China and Cochin China, 1820. Another very ornamental Crab, bearing a great abundance of rosy-pink or nearly white flowers. It is a shrub-like tree, reaching a height of 20 feet, and with an upright habit of growth. Bark of a rich, reddish-brown colour. It is one of the most profuse and persistent bloomers of the whole family.

P. SINENSIS (syn Cydonia chinensis).--Chinese Quince. China, 1818. This is rarely seen in cultivation, it having, comparatively speaking, few special merits of recommendation.

P. SMITHII (syns Mespilis Smithii and *M. grandiflora*).--Smith's Medlar. Caucasus, 1800. The habit of this tree closely resembles that of a Hawthorn, and although the flowers are only half the size of those of the Common Medlar, they are produced in greater profusion, so that the round-headed tree becomes a sheet of white blossom during May and June. The reddish-brown fruits are small for a Medlar, and ripen in October.

P. TORMINALIS.--Wild Service Tree. A native species of small growth, with ovate-cordate leaves, and small white flowers. P. torminalis pinnatifida, with acutely-lobed leaves, and oval-oblong fruit may just be mentioned.

P. VESTITA.--Nepaul White Beam. Nepaul, 1820. In this species the leaves are very large, ovate-acute or elliptic, and when young thickly coated with a white woolly-like substance, but which with warm weather gradually gives way until they are of a smooth and shining green. The flowers are borne in woolly racemose corymbs, and are white succeeded by greenish-brown berries as large as marbles.

Other species of less interest are P. varidosa, P. salicifolia, P. salvaefolia, P. Bollwylleriana, and P. Amygdaliformis. They are all of free growth, and the readiest culture, and being perfectly hardy are well worthy of a much larger share of attention than they have heretofore received.

RHAMNUS.

RHAMNUS ALATERNUS.--Mediterranean region, 1629. This is an evergreen shrub, with lanceolate shining leaves of a dark glossy-green colour, and pretty flowers produced from March till June. There are several well-marked varieties, one with golden and another with silvery leaves, and named respectively, R. Alaternus foliis aureis, and R. Alaternus foliis argenteus.

R. ALPINUS.--Europe, 1752. This is a neat-growing species, with greenish flowers and black fruit.

R. CATHARTICUS, Common Buckthorn, is a native, thorny species, with ovate and stalked leaves, and small, thickly clustered greenish flowers, succeeded by black berries about the size of peas.

R. FRANGULA.--The Berry-bearing Alder. Europe and Britain. A more erect shrub than the former, and destitute of spines. The leaves too are larger, and the fruit of a dark purple colour when ripe. More common in Britain than the former.

RHAPHIOLEPIS.

RHAPHIOLEPIS JAPONICA INTEGERRIMA (syn R. ovata).--A Japanese shrub (1865), with deep green, ovate, leathery leaves that are not over abundant, and produced generally at the branch-tips. The pure white, fragrant flowers are plentifully produced when the plant is grown in a cosy corner, or on a sunny wall. Though seldom killed outright, the Raphiolepis becomes badly crippled in severe winters. It is, however, a bold and handsome shrub, and one that may be seen doing well in many gardens around London.

RHAPHITHAMNUS.

RHAPHITHAMNUS CYANOCARPUS (syn Citharexylum cyanocarpum). Chili. This bears a great resemblance to some of the thorny Berberis, and is at once a distinct and beautiful shrub. The flowers are large and conspicuous, and of a taking bluish-lilac colour. Having stood unharmed in Ireland through the unusually severe winters of 1879-80, when many more common shrubs were killed outright, it may be relied upon as at least fairly hardy. The soil in which this rare and pretty shrub does best is a brown, fibrous peat, intermingled with sharp sand.

RHODODENDRON.

RHODODENDRON ARBORESCENS (syn Azalea arborescens), from the Carolina Mountains (1818), is a very showy, late-blooming species. The white, fragrant flowers, and noble port, together with its undoubted hardihood, should make this shrub a general favourite with cultivators.

R. CALENDULACEUM (syn Azalea calendulacea), from North America (1806), is another of the deciduous species, having oblong, hairy leaves, and large orange-coloured flowers. It is of robust growth, and in favoured situations reaches a height of 6 feet. When in full flower the slopes of the Southern Alleghany Mountains are rendered highly attractive by reason of the great flame-coloured masses of this splendid plant, and are one of the great sights of the American Continent during the month of June.

R. CALIFORNICUM.--California. A good hardy species with broadly campanulate rosy-purple flowers, spotted with yellow.

R. CAMPANULATUM (syn R. aeruginosum).--Sikkim, 1825. A small-growing species, rarely over 6 feet high, with elliptic leaves that are fawn-coloured on the under sides. The campanulate flowers are large and showy, rose or white and purple spotted, at the base of the three upper lobes. In this country it is fairly hardy, but suffers in very severe weather, unless planted in a sheltered site.

R. CAMPYLOCARPUM.--Sikkim, 1851. This has stood the winter uninjured in so many districts that it may at least be recommended for planting in favoured situations and by the seaside. It is a Sikkim species that was introduced about forty years ago, and is still rather rare. The leaves are about 4 inches long, 2 inches wide, and distinctly undulated on the margins. Flowers bell-shaped, about 2 inches in diameter, and arranged in rather straggling terminal heads. They are sulphur-yellow, without markings, a tint distinct from any other known Indian species.

R. CATAWBIENSE.--Mountains from Virginia to Georgia, 1809. A bushy, free growing species, with broadly oval leaves, and large campanulate flowers, produced in compact, rounded clusters. They vary a good deal in colour, but lilac-purple is the typical shade. This is a very valuable species, and one that has given rise to a large number of beautiful varieties.

R. CHRYSANTHUM is a Siberian species (1796) of very dwarf, compact growth, with linear-lanceolate leaves that are ferruginous on the under side, and beautiful golden-yellow flowers an inch in diameter. It is a desirable but scarce species.

R. COLLETTIANUM is an Afghanistan species, and one that may be reckoned upon as being perfectly hardy. It is of very dwarf habit, and bears an abundance of small white and faintly fragrant flowers. For planting on rockwork it is a valuable species.

R. DAHURICUM.--Dahuria, 1780. A small-growing, scraggy-looking species of about a yard high, with oval-oblong leaves that are rusty-tomentose on the under sides. The flowers, which are produced in February, are purple or violet, in twos or threes, and usually appear before the leaves. It is a sparsely-leaved species, and of greatest value on account of the flowers being produced so early in the season. One of the hardiest species in cultivation. R. dahuricum atro-virens is a beautiful and worthy variety because nearly evergreen.

R. FERRUGINEUM.--Alpine Rose. Europe, 1752. This dwarf species, rarely exceeding a yard in height, occurs in abundance on the Swiss Alps, and generally where few other plants are to be found. It is a neat little compact shrub, with oblong-lanceolate leaves that are rusty-scaly on the under sides, and has terminal clusters of rosy-red flowers.

R. FLAVUM (syn Azalea pontica).--Pontic Azalea. A native of Asia Minor (1793), is probably the commonest of the recognised species, and may frequently, in this country, be seen forming good round bushes of 6 feet in height, with hairy lanceolate leaves, and large yellow flowers, though in this latter it varies considerably, orange, and orange tinged with red, being colours often present. It is of free growth in any good light peaty or sandy soil.

R. HIRSUTUM.--Alpine Rose. South Europe, 1656. Very near R. ferrugincum, but having ciliated leaves, with glands on both sides. R. hallense and R. hirsutiforme are intermediate forms of a natural cross between R. hirsutum and R. ferrugincum. They are handsome, small-growing, brightly flowered plants, and worthy of culture.

R. INDICUM.--Indian Azalea. A native of China (1808), and perfectly hardy in the more favoured portions of southern England, where it looks healthy and happy out of doors, and blooms freely from year to year. This is the evergreen so-called Azalea that is so commonly cultivated in greenhouses, with long hirsute leaves, and large showy flowers. R. indicum amoenum (syn Azalea amoena), as a greenhouse plant is common enough, but except in the South of England and Ireland it is not sufficiently hardy to withstand severe frost. The flowers are, moreover, not very showy, at least when compared with some of the newer forms, being dull magenta, and rather lax of habit.

R. LEDIFOLIUM (syns Azalea ledifolia and *A. liliiflora*).--Ledum-leaved Azalea. China, 1819. A perfectly hardy species. The flowers are large and white, but somewhat flaunting. It is, however, a desirable species for massing in quantity, beside clumps of the pink and yellow flowered kinds. Though introduced nearly three-quarters of a century ago, this is by no means a common plant in our gardens.

R. MAXIMUM.--American Great Laurel. North America, 1756. This is a very hardy American species, growing in favoured localities from 10 feet to 15 feet high. Leaves oblong-lanceolate, slightly ferruginous beneath. Flowers rose and white, in dense clusters. There are several handsome varieties that vary to a wide extent in the size and colour of flowers. R. maximum album bears white flowers.

R. MOLLE (syn Azalea mollis), from Japan (1867), is a dwarf, deciduous species of neat growth, with flame-coloured flowers. It is very hardy, and a desirable acquisition to any collection of small-growing shrubs.

R. OCCIDENTALE (syn Azalea occidentalis), Western Azalea, is valuable in that the flowers are produced later than those of almost any other species. These are white, blotched with yellow at the base of the upper petals; and being produced when the leaves are almost fully developed, have a very pleasing effect, particularly as they are borne in great quantity, and show well above the foliage. This is a Californian species that has been found further west of the Rocky Mountains than any other member of Ihe family.

R. PARVIFOLIUM.--Baiacul, 1877. This is a pleasing and interesting species, with small deep-green ovate leaves, and clusters of white flowers, margined with rose. It is of dwarf and neat growth, and well suited for planting on the rock garden.

R. PONTICUM.--Pontic Rhododendron, or Rose Bay. Asia Minor, 1763. This is the commonest species in cultivation, and although originally a native of the district by the Black or Pontic Sea, is now naturalised in many parts of Europe. It is the hardiest and least exacting of the large flowered species, and is generally employed as a stock on which to graft the less hardy kinds. Flowers, in the typical species, pale purplish-violet and spotted. There is a great number of varieties, including white, pink, scarlet, and double-flowering.

R. PONTICUM AZALEOIDES (syn R. ponticum deciduum), a hybrid between R. ponticum and a hardy Azalea, is a sub-evergreen form, with a compact habit of growth, and bearing loose heads of fragrant lavender-and-white flowers. It is quite hardy at Kew.

R. RACEMOSUM.--Central China, 1880. A neat little species, of dwarf, compact growth, from the Yunnan district of China. The flowers are pale pink edged with a deeper tint, about an inch across, and borne in terminal and axillary clusters. It has stood unharmed for several years in southern England, so may be regarded as at least fairly hardy. Its neat dwarf growth, and flowering as it does when hardly a foot high, renders it a choice subject for the Alpine garden.

R. RHODORA (syn Rhodora canadensis).--North America, 1767. In general aspect this shrub resembles an Azalea, but it comes into flower long even before R. molle. Being deciduous, and producing its pretty purplish sweet-scented flowers in early spring, gives to the plant a particular value for gardening purposes, clumps of the shrub being most effective at the very time when flowers are at their scarcest. It thrives well in any peaty soil, and is quite hardy.

R. VISCOSUM (syn Azalea viscosa).--Clammy Azalea, or Swamp Honeysuckle. North America, 1734. This is one of the hardiest, most floriferous, and easily managed of the family. The white or rose and deliciously fragrant flowers are produced in great abundance, and impart when at their best quite a charm to the shrub. It delights in rather moist, peaty soil, and grows all the stronger and flowers all the more freely when surrounded by rising ground or tall trees at considerable distance away. The variety R. viscosum glaucum has leaves paler than those of the species; and R. viscosum nitidum, of dwarf, compact growth, has leaves deep green on both sides.

R. WILSONI, a cross between R. ciliatum and R. glaucum, is of remarkably neat growth, and worthy of cultivation where small-sized kinds are a desideratum.

The following Himalayan species have been found to thrive well in the warmer parts of England, and in close proximity to the sea;--R. argenteum, R. arboreum, R. Aucklandii, R. barbatum, R. ciliatum, R. campanulatum, R. cinnabarinum, R. Campbelli, R. compylocarpum, R. eximium, R. Fortunei, R. Falconeri, R. glaucum, R. Hodgsoni, R. lanatum, R. niveum, R. Roylei, R. Thompsoni, and R. Wallichii.

R. Ungernii and R. Smirnowii, from the Armenian frontier, are also worthy of culture, but they are at present rare in cultivation in this country.

Few hardy shrubs, it must be admitted, are more beautiful than these Rhododendrons, none flowering more freely or lasting longer in bloom. Their requirements are by no means hard to meet, light, peaty soil, or even good sandy loam, with a small admixture of decayed vegetable matter, suiting them well. Lime in any form must, however, be kept away both from Azaleas and Rhododendrons. They like a quiet, still place, where a fair amount of moisture is present in the air and soil.

HARDY HYBRID RHODODENDRONS.

GHENT AZALEAS, as generally known, from having been raised in Belgium, are a race of hybrids that have been produced by crossing the Asiatic R. pontica with the various American species noted above, but particularly R. calendulaceum, R. nudiflorum, and R. viscosum, and these latter with one another. These have produced hybrids of almost indescribable beauty, the flowers of which range in colour from crimson and pink, through orange and yellow, to almost white.

Within the last few years quite an interesting race of Rhododendrons has been brought out, with double or hose-in-hose flowers, and very appropriately termed the Narcissiflora group. They include fully a dozen highly ornamental kinds, with flowers of varying shades of colour.

The following list includes some of the best and most beautiful of these varieties:--

Alba marginata.
Ardens.
Astreans.
Aurore-de-Royghen.
Baron G. Pyke.
BeautE Celeste.
Bessie Holdaway.
Belle Merveille.
Bijou des Amateurs.
Cardinal.
Charles Bowman.
Comte de Flanders.
Decus hortorum.
Due de Provence.
Emperor Napoleon III.

Eugenie.
Fitz Quihou.
Glorie de Belgique.
Gloria Mundi.
Gueldres Rose.
Honneur de Flandre.
Imperator.
Jules Caesar.
La Superbe.
Louis Hellebuyck.
Madame Baumann.
Marie Verschaffelt.
Mathilde.
Meteor.
Nancy Waterer.
Ne Plus Ultra.
Optima.
Pallas.
Queen Victoria.
Reine des Belges.
Remarquable.
Roi des Belges.
Roi des Feux.
Sinensis rosea.
Sulphurea.
Triumphans.
Unique.
Viscocephala.

Double-flowered Rhododendrons:--

Bijou de Gendbrugge.
Graf Von Meran.

Heroine.
Narcissiflora.
Louis AimEe Van Houtte.
Mina Van Houtte.
OphiriE.
Van Houttei.

RHODOTHAMNUS.

RHODOTHAMNUS CHAMAECISTUS (syn Rhododendron Chamaecistus).--Ground Cistus. Alps of Austria and Bavaria, 1786. A very handsome shrub, of small growth, and widely distributed in Bavaria, Switzerland, and elsewhere. Planted in peaty soil and in a rather damp, shady situation it thrives best, the oval-serrate leaves, covered with white, villous hairs, and pretty rosy flowers, giving it an almost unique appearance. It is a charming rock shrub and perfectly hardy.

RHODOTYPOS.

RHODOTYPOS KERRIOIDES.--White Kerria. Japan, 1866. A handsome deciduous shrub, and one that is readily propagated, and comparatively cheap. It is distinct and pretty when in flower, and one of the hardiest and most accommodating of shrubs. The leaves are handsome, being deeply serrated and silky on the under sides, while the pure white flowers are often about 2 inches across. It grows about 4 feet in height, and is a very distinct and desirable shrub.

RHUS.

RHUS COTINUS.--Smoke Plant, Wig Tree, or Venetian Sumach. Spain to Caucasus, 1656. On account of its singular appearance this shrub always attracts the attention of even the most unobservant in such matters. It is a spreading shrub, about 6 feet high, with rotundate, glaucous leaves, on long petioles. The flowers are small and inconspicuous, but the feathery nature of the flower clusters, occasioned by the transformation of the pedicels and hairs into fluffy awns, renders this Sumach one of the most curious and attractive of hardy shrubs. Spreading about freely, this south European shrub should be allowed plenty of room so that it may become perfectly developed.

R. GLABRA (syns R. caroliniana, R. coccinea, R. elegans, and *R. sanguinea*).--Smooth or Scarlet Sumach. North America, 1726. A smaller tree than the last, with leaves that are deep glossy-green above and whitish beneath. The male tree bears greenish-yellow flowers, and the female those of a reddish-scarlet, but otherwise no difference between the trees can be detected. R. glabra laciniata (Fern Sumach) is a distinct and handsome variety, with finely cut elegant leaves, and a dwarf and compact habit of growth. The leaves are very beautiful, and resemble those of the Grevillea robusta. It is a worthy variety.

R. SUCCEDANEA.--Red Lac Sumach. Japan, 1768. This is not often seen planted out, though in not a few places it succeeds perfectly well. It has elegant foliage, each leaf being 15 inches long, and divided into several pairs of leaflets.

R. TOXICODENDRON.--Poison Oak or Poison Ivy. North America, 1640. This species is of half-scandent habit, with large, trifoliolate leaves, which turn of various tints of red and crimson in the autumn. It is quite hardy, and seen to best advantage when allowed to run over large rockwork and tree stumps in partial shade. The variety R. toxicodendron radicans has ample foliage, and is suited for similar places to the last. The leaves turn bright yellow in the autumn.

R. TYPHINA.--Stag's Horn Sumach, or Vinegar Tree. A native of North America (1629), and a very common shrub in our gardens, probably on account of its spreading rapidly by suckers. It is, when well grown, a handsome and distinct shrub or small tree, with large, pinnate, hairy leaves, and shoots that are rendered very peculiar by reason of the dense hairs with which they are covered for some distance back. The dense clusters of greenish-yellow flowers are sure to attract attention, although they are by no means pretty. R. typhina viridiflora is the male-flowered form of this species, with green flowers.

R. VENENATA (syn R. vernix).--Poison Elder, Sumach, or Dogwood. North America, 1713. This is remarkable for its handsome foliage, and is the most poisonous species of the genus.

All the Sumachs grow and flower freely in any good garden soil, indeed, in that respect they are not at all particular. They throw up shoots freely, so that increasing the stock is by no means difficult.

RIBES.

RIBES ALPINUM PUMILUM AUREUM.--Golden Mountain Currant. The ordinary green form is a native of Britain, of which the plant named above is a dwarf golden-leaved variety.

R. AUREUM.--Buffalo Currant. North-west America, 1812. In this species the leaves are lobed and irregularly toothed, while the flowers are yellow, or slightly reddish-tinted. It is of rather slender and straggling growth. R. aureum praecox is an early-flowering variety; and R. aureum serotinum is valued on account of the flowers being produced much later than are those of the parent plant.

R. CEREUM (syn R. inebrians).--North America, 1827. One of the dwarfer-growing species of Flowering Currant, forming a low, dense bush of Gooseberry-like appearance, but destitute of spines. By May it is in full flower, and the blooms, borne in large clusters, have a pretty pinkish tinge. The foliage is small, neat, and of a tender green that helps to set off the pretty flowers to perfection. It is a native of North-west America, and perfectly hardy in every part of the country. Though not equal in point of floral beauty with our common flowering Currant, still the miniature habit, pretty and freely-produced pink-tinted flowers, and fresh green foliage will all help to make it an acquisition wherever planted. Like the other species of Ribes the present plant grows and flowers very freely in any soil, and almost however poor.

R. FLORIDUM (syns R. missouriense and *R. pennsylvanicum*).--American Wild Black Currant. North America, 1729. This should be included in all collections for its pretty autumnal foliage, which is of a bright purplish bronze.

R. GORDONIANUM (syns R. Beatonii and *R. Loudonii*) is a hybrid between R. aureum and R. sanguineum, and has reddish, yellow tinged flowers, and partakes generally of the characters of both species.

R. MULTIFLORUM, Eastern Europe (1822), is another desirable species, with long drooping racemes of greenish-yellow flowers, and small red berries.

R. SANGUINEUM.--Flowering Currant. North-west America, 1826. An old inhabitant of our gardens, and well deserving of all that can be said in its favour as a beautiful spring-flowering shrub. It is of North American origin, with deep red and abundantly-produced flowers. There are several distinct varieties as follows:--R. sanguineum flore-pleno (Burning Bush), with perfectly double flowers, which are produced later and last longer than those of the species; R. sanguineum album, with pale pink, or almost white flowers; R. sanguineum atro-rubens, with deeply-coloured flowers; R. sanguineum glutinosum and R. sanguineum grandiflorum, bearing compact clusters of flowers that are rosy-flesh coloured on the outside and white or pinky-white within.

R. SPECIOSUM.--Fuchsia-flowered Gooseberry. California, 1829. A Californian species, remarkable for being more or less spiny, and with flowers resembling some of the Fuchsias. They are crimson, and with long, protruding stamens. As a wall plant, where it often rises to 6 feet in height, this pretty and taking species is most often seen.

The flowering Currants are of unusually free growth, and are not at all particular about soil, often thriving well in that of a very poor description. They are increased readily from cuttings and by layers.

ROBINIA.

ROBINIA DUBIA (syns R. echiuata and **R. ambigua**).--A very pretty garden hybrid form, said to have for its parentage R. Pseud-Acacia and R. viscosa. It is of quite tree-like growth and habit, with unusually short spines, and Pea-green foliage. The flowers are produced pretty freely, and are of a pale rose colour, and well set off by the light-green leaves, over which they hang in neat and compact spikes.

R. HISPIDA.--Rose Acacia. North America, 1743. Amongst large-growing shrubs this is certainly one of the most distinct and handsome, and at the same time one of the hardiest and readiest of culture. Under favourable conditions it grows about 16 feet high, with large oval or oblong leaflets, and having the young branches densely clothed with bristles. The flowers, which are individually larger than those of the False Acacia, are of a beautiful rosy-pink, and produced in June and July. It is a very ornamental, small growing species, and one that is peculiarly suitable for planting where space is limited. R. hispida macrophylla (Large-leaved Rose Acacia) is rendered distinct by its generally more robust growth, and by its larger foliage and flowers. The species, however, varies a good deal in respect of the size of leaves and flowers.

R. PSEUD-ACACIA.--Common Locust, Bastard Acacia, or False Acacia. North America, 1640. A noble-growing and handsome tree, with smooth shoots, and stipules that become transformed into sharp, stiff spines. The flowers are in long racemes, pure-white or slightly tinged with pink, and with a faint pleasing odour. This species has been sub-divided into a great number of varieties, some of which are very distinct, but the majority are not sufficiently so to warrant special attention. The following include the best and most popular kinds:--R. Pseud-Acacia Decaisneana, a distinct form bearing light pinky flowers; R. Pseud-Acacia Bessoniana, with thornless branches and a dense head of refreshing Pea-green foliage; R. Pseud-Acacia angustifolia, with narrow leaves; R. Pseud-Acacia aurea, a conspicuous but not very constant golden leaved form; R. Pseud-Acacia inermis, of which there are weeping, upright, and broad-leaved forms, has narrow leaves that are glaucous beneath, and the characteristic spines of the species are wanting or rarely well developed. R. Pseud-Acacia monophylla is very distinct, the leaves being entire instead of pinnate; while R. Pseud-Acacia crispa has curiously-curled foliage. Then there is the peculiar R. Pseud-Acacia tortuosa, of ungainly habit; R. Pseud-Acacia umbraculifera, with a spreading head; R. Pseud-Acacia sophoraefolia, the leaves of which resemble those of Sophora japonica; and R. Pseud-Acacia amorphaefolia, with very large foliage when compared with the parent tree. The above may be taken as the most distinct and desirable forms of the False Acacia, but there are many others, such as R. Pseud-Acacia colutoides,

R. Pseud-Acacia semperflorens, and R. Pseud-Acacia Rhederi, all more or less distinct from the typical tree.

R. VISCOSA (syn R. glutinosa).--Clammy Locust. North America, 1797. This is a small-growing tree, and readily distinguished by the clammy bark of the younger shoots. Flowers in short racemes, and of a beautiful rose-pink, but varying a good deal in depth of tint. It is a valuable species for ornamental planting, and flowers well even in a young state.

Few soils would seem to come amiss to the Acacias, but observations made in many parts of the country conclusively prove that the finest specimens are growing on light, rich loam overlying a bed of gravel. They are propagated from seed, by layers, or by grafting.

ROSA.

ROSA ALBA.--This is a supposed garden hybrid between R. canina and R. gallica (1597). It has very glaucous foliage, and large flowers, which vary according to the variety from pure white to rose.

R. REPENS (syn R. arvensis).--Field Rose. Europe (Britain). This species bears white flowers that are produced in threes or fours, rarely solitary. The whole plant is usually of weak and straggling growth, with shining leaves.

R. BRACTEATA (Macartney Rose), R. PALUSTRIS (Marsh Rose), and R. MICROPHYLLA (small-leaved Rose), belong to that section supplied with floral leaves or bracts, and shaggy fruit. They are of compact growth, with neat, shining leaves, the flowers of the first-mentioned being rose or carmine, and those of the other two pure white.

R. CANINA.--Dog Rose. Our native Roses have now been reduced to five species, of which the present is one of the number. It is a straggling shrub, 6 feet or 8 feet high, and armed with curved spines. Flowers sweet-scented, pink or white, and solitary, or in twos or threes at the branch tips.

R. CENTIFOLIA.--Hundred-leaved, or Cabbage Rose. Orient, 1596. A beautiful, sweetly-scented species, growing to 6 feet in height, and having leaves that are composed of from three to five broadly ovate, toothed leaflets. The flowers are solitary, or two or three together, drooping, and of a rosy hue, but differing in tint to a considerable extent. This species has varied very much, principally through the influences of culture and crossing, the three principal and marked variations being size, colour, and clothing of the calyx tube. There are the common Provence Roses, the miniature Provence or Pompon Roses, and the Moss Rose--all of which are merely races of R. centifolia.

R. DAMASCENA.--Damask Rose. Orient, 1573. A bushy shrub varying from 2 feet to 8 feet in height according to cultural treatment and age. The flowers are white or red, large, borne in corymbose clusters, and produced in great profusion during June and July. The varieties that have arisen under cultivation by seminal variation, hybridisation, or otherwise are exceedingly numerous. Those now grown are mostly double, and a large proportion of them are light in colour. They include the quatre saisons and the true York and Lancaster. The flowers are highly fragrant, and, like those of R. centifolia and other species, are used indiscriminately for the purpose of making rose water. The species is distinguished from R. centifolia by its larger prickles, elongated fruit, and long, reflexed sepals.

R. FEROX.--North Asia. This species bears flowers in clusters of two and three together, terminating the branches. The petals are white with a yellow base. The branches are erect, and thickly crowded with prickles of unequal size.

R. GALLICA.--The French, or Gallic Rose. Europe and Western Asia. This Rose forms a bushy shrub 2 feet to 3 feet high, and has been so long grown in British gardens that the date of its introduction has been lost in obscurity. It is doubtless the red Rose of ancient writers, but at present the flowers may be red, crimson, or white, and there are varieties of all intermediate shades. Several variegated or striped Roses belong here, including Gloria Mundi, a popular favourite often but erroneously grown under the name of York and Lancaster. They all flower in June and July, and, together with other kinds that flower about the same time, are generally known as summer or old-fashioned garden Roses.

R. HEMISPHAERICA (syn R. sulphurea).--Orient, 1629. A bushy plant growing from 4 feet to 6 feet high, and bearing large double yellow flowers.

R. INDICA.--Common China, or Monthly Rose. Introduced from China, near Canton, in 1789, but the native country is not known with certainty. The flowers of the plant when first introduced were red and generally semi-double, but the varieties now vary through all shades of blush, rose, and crimson, and the plant varies exceedingly in height, in its different forms 1 foot to 20 feet in height. The Monthly Roses form bushes generally about 2 feet high or a little over. The Noisette and Tea Roses, with several other more or less distinct types, belong here, but as most of them are well known and otherwise well cared for, it is unnecessary to dwell upon them in detail beyond the two varieties here given, and which should not be overlooked.

R. INDICA MINIMA (syn R. semperflorens minima, R. Lawrenceana, and *R. minima*).--Fairy, or Miniature Rose. China, 1810. A beautiful little Rose that rarely exceeds a height of 4 inches or 5 inches. The flowers are about the size of a half-crown, and somewhat after the York and Lancaster as regards colouring, though not, perhaps, so distinctly marked, and are produced in abundance. For the rock garden it is one of the most desirable, and being perfectly hardy still further adds to its value.

R. INDICA SEMPERFLORENS (syns R. bengalensis and *R. diversifolia*).--The Ever-flowering China Rose. China, 1789. A somewhat spreading bush, with slender branches, armed with curved prickles. Leaves composed of three or five leaflets, and tinted with purple. Flowers almost scentless, solitary, semi-double, and of a bright and showy crimson.

R. LUTEA (syn R. Eglanteria).--The Austrian Brier, or Yellow Eglantine. South Europe, 1596. This belongs to the Sweet Brier section, and is a bush of from 3 feet to 6 feet high, with shining dark-green leaves, and large, cup-shaped flowers that are yellow or sometimes tinged with reddish-brown within. The Scarlet Austrian Brier (R. lutea punicea) is a handsome variety, with the upper surface of the petals scarlet and the under surface yellow.

R. RUBIGINOSA (syn R. Eglanteria).--Eglantine, or Sweet Brier. This species has pink flowers and clammy leaves, which are glandular on the under surface, and give out a fragrant smell by which it may be recognised.

R. RUGOSA (syn R. ferox of Bot. Reg.), a Japanese species, and its variety R. rugosa alba, are beautiful shrubs that have proved themselves perfectly hardy and well suited for extensive culture in this country. They are of stiff, shrubby habit, about 4 feet high, and with branches thickly clothed with spines becoming brown with age. Leaflets oval in shape, deep green, with the upper surface rough to the touch, the under sides densely tomentose. Flowers single, fully 3 inches in diameter, the petals of good substance, and white or rose-coloured. The fruit is large, larger than that of perhaps any other rose, and of a bright red when fully ripe. In so far as beauty of fruit is concerned, this Rose has certainly no rival, and whether for the rockwork or open border it must be classed amongst the most useful and beautiful of hardy shrubs. R. rugosa is a capital hedge plant, and being a true species it is readily propagated from seed. R. rugosa Kamtschatika is a deep-red flowered form with deciduous spines.

R. SEMPERVIRENS.--Evergreen Rose. South Europe and India, 1529. A climbing species, with long, slender branches, armed with hooked prickles. Leaves evergreen, shining, and composed of from five to seven leaflets. The clustered flowers are white and sweet-scented.

R. SPINOSISSIMA (syn R. pimpinellifolia).--Burnet, or Scotch Rose. A small bush about 2 feet high, of neat growth, with small leaves, and pink or white flowers that are solitary at the branch ends.

R. VILLOSA.--Downy Rose. Europe (Britain). This species is of erect bushy growth, with the leaflets softly downy on both sides. Flowers white or pale pink, succeeded by globular fruits, that are more or less covered with fine hair or prickles.

ROSMARINUS.

ROSMARINUS OFFICINALIS.--Common Rosemary. Mediterranean region, 1848. A familiar garden shrub, of dense growth, with dusky-gray green linear leaves, and pale blue or white flowers. There is a golden and a silver leaved variety, named respectively R. officinalis foliis-aureis, and R. officinalis foliis-argenteis; as also one distinguished by having broader foliage than the species, and named R. officinalis latifolius.

RUBUS.

RUBUS ARCTICUS.--Arctic Regions of both hemispheres. An interesting species about 6 inches high, with trifoliolate leaves, and deep-red flowers. For Alpine gardening it is a valuable species of dwarf growth.

R. AUSTRALIS, from New Zealand, is a very prickly species, with the leaves reduced to their stalks and the midribs of three leaflets. Not being very hardy it is usually seen as a wall plant.

R. BIFLORUS.--Himalayas, 1818. A tall-growing species with whitish, spiny stems, and simple three-lobed leaves that are tomentose on the under sides. The flowers are thickly produced, pure white, and render the plant highly attractive, and of great beauty.

R. DELICIOSUS.--This Rocky Mountain Bramble (1870) is a very worthy species, with three or five-lobed (not pinnate) leaves, and large, pure white flowers that are each about 2 inches in diameter, and produced in profusion from the leaf-axils. For ornamental planting this may be placed in the first rank of the family to which it belongs.

R. FRUTICOSUS.--Common Bramble, or Blackberry. Of this well-known native species there are several worthy varieties, of which the double-flowered are especially worth notice, blooming as they do in the latter part of summer. R. fruticosus flore albo-pleno (Double white-flowered Bramble), and R. fruticosus flore roseo-pleno (Double red-flowered Bramble) are very pretty and showy varieties, and well worth including in any collection. There is a pretty variegated-leaved form of the common Bramble, known as R. fruticosus variegatus.

R. LACINIATUS, Cut-leaved Bramble, might also be included on account of its profusion of white flowers, and neatly divided foliage.

R. NUTKANUS.--North America, 1826. This has white flowers, but otherwise it resembles R. odoratus.

R. ODORATUS.--Purple flowering Raspberry. North America, 1700. The sweet-scented Virginian Raspberry forms a rather dense, upright growing bush, fully 4 feet high, with large broadly five-lobed and toothed leaves, that are more or less viscid, sweet-scented, and deciduous. The leaves are placed on long, hairy, viscid foot-stalks. Flowers in terminal corymbs, large and nearly circular, purplish-red in colour, and composed of five broad, round petals. The fruit, which is rarely produced in this country, is velvety and amber-coloured. It is a very ornamental species, the ample Maple-like leaves and large flowers rendering it particularly attractive in summer. The leaves, and not the flowers as is generally supposed, are sweetly scented.

R. ROSAEFOLIUS.--Rose-leaved Raspberry. Himalayas, 1811. Another half-hardy species, and only suited for planting against sunny walls. Leaves pinnate, finer than those of the Raspberry. R. r. coronarius, with semi-double white flowers, is better than the type.

R. SPECTABILIS.--The Salmon Berry. North America, 1827. Grows about 6 feet high, with ternate or tri-lobate leaves that are very thickly produced. Flowers usually bright red or purplish-coloured, and placed on long pendulous footstalks. It is of very dense growth, occasioned by the number of suckers sent up from the roots.

There are also some of the so-called American Brambles well worthy of attention, two of the best being Kittatiny and Lawton's:

The brambles are particularly valuable shrubs, as owing to their dense growth they may be used for a variety of purposes, but especially for covering unsightly objects or banks. They are all wonderfully floriferous, and succeed admirably even in very poor and stony soils.

Increase is readily obtained either from root suckers or by layering.

RUSCUS.

RUSCUS ACULEATUS.--Butcher's Broom, Pettigree and Pettigrue. Europe (Britain), and North Africa. This is a native evergreen shrub, with rigid cladodes which take the place of leaves, and not very showy greenish flowers appearing about May. For the bright red berries, which are as large as small marbles, it is alone worth cultivating, while it is one of the few shrubs that grow at all satisfactorily beneath the shade of our larger trees.

R. HYPOPHYLLUM.--Double Tongue. Mediterranean region, 1640. This species has the flowers on the undersides of the leaf-like branches; and its variety R.H. Hypoglossum has them on the upper side. Both are of value for planting in the shade.

SAMBUCUS.

SAMBUCUS CALIFORNICA.--Californian Elder. A rare species as yet, but one
that from its elegant growth and duration of flowers is sure, when better known, to become widely distributed.

S. GLAUCA has its herbaceous parts covered with a thick pubescence; leaves pubescent on both sides, and with yellow flowers produced in umbels.

S. NIGRA.--Common Elder. Bourtry, or Bour tree. Although one of our commonest native trees, the Elder must rank amongst the most ornamental if only for its large compound cymes of white or yellowish-white flowers, and ample bunches of shining black berries. There are, however, several varieties that should be largely cultivated, such as S. nigra foliis aureis (Golden Elder), S. nigra fructu albo (White Fruited), S. nigra laciniata (Cut-leaved Elder), S. nigra argentea (Silver-leaved Elder), S. nigra rotundifolia (Round-leaved Elder), the names of which will be sufficient for the purposes of recognition.

S. RACEMOSA.--Scarlet-berried Elder. South Europe and Siberia, 1596. This is almost a counterpart of our native species, but instead of black the berries are brilliant scarlet. It is a highly ornamental species, but it is rather exacting, requiring for its perfect growth a cool and moist situation. Of this there is a cut-leaved, form, named S. racemosa serratifolia.

S. ROSAEFLORA is said to be a seedling from S. glauca, but differs in many important points from the parent. It has smooth shoots and branches, ovate-acuminate leaves that are downy beneath, and flowers rose-coloured without and white within. They are produced in short, spike-like clusters, and are almost destitute of smell. The reddish rings at the insertion of the leaves is another distinguishing feature.

For freedom of growth in almost every class of soil, and readiness with which they may be increased, the more showy kinds of Elder are well worthy of attention.

SCHIZANDRA.

SCHIZANDRA CHINENSIS.--Northern China, 1860. This is a climbing shrub, with oval, bright green leaves, and showy carmine flowers. For clothing arbors and walls it may prove of use, but it is as yet rare in cultivation.

S. COCCINEA, from North America (1806), is another uncommon species in which the leaves are oblong and petiolate, and the flowers red or scarlet. For purposes similar to the last this species may be employed.

SCHIZOPHRAGMA.

SCHIZOPHRAGMA HYDRANGEOIDES.--Climbing Hydrangea. Japan, 1879. As yet this is an uncommon shrub, and allied to the Hydrangea. It is of slender growth, the stems rooting into the support, and with pinky-white flowers. As an ornamental climber it is of no great value, and requires a favoured spot to grow it at all satisfactorily.

SHEPHERDIA.

SHEPHERDIA ARGENTEA.--Beef Suet Tree, or Rabbit Berry. North America, 1820. This shrub is rendered of particular interest on account of the intense silvery hue of the foliage. The leaves are narrow and lanceolate, silvery on both sides, and dotted over with rusty-brown scales beneath. The flowers, which are produced in April, are small and yellow, unisexual, or each sex on a distinct plant. Berries scarlet, about the size of red Currants, and ripe about September.

S. CANADENSIS.--North America, 1759. This is a small-growing, straggling species, fully 4 feet high, and clothed with rusty scales. The leaves are ovate or elliptic, and green above, and the flowers of an inconspicuous yellow, succeeded by orange-red berries.

SKIMMIA.

SKIMMIA FORTUNEI.--Japan, 1845. This is a neat-growing shrub, with glossy, laurel-like leaves, white or greenish-white flowers, and an abundance of scarlet berries in autumn. It succeeds best in a somewhat shady situation, and when planted in not too heavy peaty soil, but where abundance of not stagnant moisture is present.

S. JAPONICA (of Thunberg) (syn S. oblata).--Japan, 1864. A neat-growing, evergreen shrub, with rather larger and more showy leaves than the former, and spikes of pretty whitish, sweetly scented flowers. The female form of this is usually known as S. fragrans. What is usually known as S. oblata ovata, and S. oblata Veitchii, are only forms of the true S. japonica; while S. fragrantissima is the male of the same species. The beautiful, berried plant that has been exhibited under the name of S. Foremanii, and which is of very vigorous growth, and produces pyramidal spikes of sweetly scented flowers, is probably S. japonica, or a seminal variety. Another variety sent out under the name of S. macrophylla has unusually large leaves; and another named S. Rogersi produces fruit very abundantly.

S. LAUREOLA (syn Limonia Laureola), from the Himalayas, is an uncommon species, with very fragrant and pale yellow flowers.

S. RUBELLA (China, 1874) is another member of the family that has greenish-white, sweet-scented flowers, and which when better known will be largely planted.

SMILAX.

SMILAX ASPERA.--The Prickly Ivy. South Europe, 1648. A trailing-habited shrub, with prickly stems, ovate, spiny-toothed, evergreen leaves, and rather unattractive flowers. There are other hardy species from North America, including S. Bona-nox (better known as S. tamnoides), S. rotundifolia, and S. herbacea, the first being the most desirable. S. aspera mauritanica is a hardy variety, but one that is rare in cultivation, with long, wiry shoots, and well adapted for wall or trellis covering. They all require favoured situations, else the growth is short, and the plants stunted and meagre in appearance.

SOLANUM.

SOLANUM CRISPUM.--Potato-tree. A native of Chili, 1824, and not very hardy, except in the coast regions of England and Ireland. It grows stout and bushy, often in favoured places rising to the height of 12 feet, and has large clusters of purple-blue flowers that are succeeded by small, white berries. This is a decidedly ornamental shrub, that should be cultivated wherever a suitable place can be spared. It bears hard pruning back with impunity, and succeeds in any light, rich, loamy soil.

S. DULCAMARA.--Bitter Sweet, and Woody Nightshade. This is a native plant, and one of great beauty when seen clambering over a fence, or bank. It has long, flexuous stems, and large clusters of purple flowers, which are made all the more conspicuous by the showy yellow anthers. The scarlet fruit is very effective.

SOPHORA.

SOPHORA JAPONICA (syn Styphnolobium japonicum).--Chinese or Japanese Pagoda-tree. China and Japan, 1763. A large deciduous tree, with elegant pinnate foliage, and clusters of greenish-white flowers produced in September. Leaves dark-green, and composed of about eleven leaflets. S.

japonica pendula is one of the most constant of weeping trees, and valuable for planting in certain well-chosen spots on the lawn or in the park.

S. TETRAPTERA.--New Zealand, 1772. This requires protection in this country. It is a valuable species, having numerous leaflets, and bearing racemes of very showy yellow flowers. S. tetraptera microphylla is a smaller-leaved variety, with ten to forty pairs of leaflets, and is known in gardens under the names of Edwardsia Macnabiana, and E. tatraptera microphylla.

SPARTIUM.

SPARTIUM JUNCEUM (syn S. acutifolium).--Spanish, or Rush Broom. Mediterranean region and Canary Isles, 1548. This resembles our common Broom, but the slender Rush-like branches are not angular, and usually destitute of leaves. The fragrant yellow flowers are produced abundantly in racemes, and when at their best impart to the shrub a very striking and beautiful appearance. For planting in poor, sandy or gravelly soils, or amongst stones and shingle, and where only a very limited number of shrubs could be got to grow, the Spanish Broom will be found an excellent and valuable plant. It is a native of Southern Europe, and is quite hardy all over the country. Propagated from seed.

SPIRAEA.

SPIRAEA BELLA.--Pretty-flowered Spiraea. Himalayas, 1820. The reddish stems of this rather tall-growing species are of interest, and render the plant distinct. Leaves ovate, acute, and serrated, and tomentose beneath. Flowers in spreading corymbs of a very beautiful rose colour, and at their best from the middle of May till the middle of June. S.

bella alba has white flowers.

S. BLUMEI.--Blume's Spiraea. Japan. This is a Japanese species, growing 4 feet or 5 feet high, with small, ovate, bluntly-pointed leaves, and white flowers arranged in compact terminal cymes. It is a good and worthy species for ornamental planting.

S. BULLATA (syn S. crispifolia.)--Japan. This will ever be accounted valuable for the rock garden, owing to its very dwarf habit and extreme floriferousness. It bears tiny bunches of bright rose-coloured flowers, and these look all the more charming owing to the miniature size of the shrub, its average height being about 12 inches. A very interesting and valuable rock shrub, and one that no doubt about its perfect hardihood need be entertained.

S. CANA.--Hoary-leaved Spiraea. Croatia, 1825. This is a small spreading shrub that rarely rises to more than 18 inches in height, with small, ovate, hoary leaves, and pretty white flowers arranged in corymbs. For rockwork planting it is one of the most valuable species, growing freely and producing its showy flowers in abundance. Quite hardy.

S. CANTONIENSIS (syn S. Reevesiana).--Reeve's Spiraea. Japan, 1843. An evergreen or sub-evergreen species, growing 3 feet high, with lanceolate leaves on long footstalks, and large, pure white flowers arranged in terminal corymbs, and placed on long peduncles.

S. CHAMAEDRIFOLIA (syn S. ceanothifolia).--Germander-leaved Spiraea. South-eastern Europe to Japan, 1789. Grows about a yard high, with ovate, pubescent leaves, and white flowers. It varies widely in the shape and size of leaves. S. chamaedrifolia ulmifolia (Elm-leaved Spiraea) a twiggy shrub, 3 feet high, with broad leaves and white flowers, is from Siberia. S. chamaedrifolia crataegifolia (Hawthorn-leaved Spiraea) is of stout, half-erect growth, with rather stiff glaucous leaves that are oval in shape, and bright red or pink flowers in fastigiate panicles. From Siberia 1790, and flowering at mid-summer.

S. DECUMBENS (syn S. nana).--Decumbent Spiraea. Tyrol. This is the smallest-growing of the shrubby Spiraeas, rarely attaining to a greater height than 12 inches. It is a neat growing plant, with small oval leaves, and white pedunculate flowers. For planting on the rockwork or in the front line of the shrubbery, this is an invaluable shrub, and soon forms a neat and pretty specimen. It is perfectly hardy.

S. DISCOLOR ARIAEFOLIA (syn S. ariaefolia).--White Beam-leaved Spiraea. North-west America, 1827. This forms a dense, erect shrub about 6 feet high, with elliptic-oblong leaves, and clothed beneath with a whitish tomentum. The flowers are in large, terminal, slender-stalked panicles, and white or yellowish-white. It is one of the handsomest species in cultivation, the neat and yet not stiff habit, and pretty, plume-like tufts of flowers making it a general favourite with the cultivators of hardy shrubs. Flowers about mid-summer. In rich soils, and where partially shaded from cold winds, it thrives best.

S. DOUGLASII.--Douglas's Spiraea. North-west America. This has long, obovate-lanceolate leaves, that are white with down on the under surface, and bears dense, oblong, terminal panicles of rosy flowers. S. Douglasii Nobleana (Noble's Spiraea) is a variety of great beauty, growing about a yard high, with large leaves often 4 inches long, and looser panicles of purple-red flowers. Flowering in July. The variety was introduced from California in 1859.

S. FISSA.--Split-leaved Spiraea. Mexico, 1839. A stout, erect-growing shrub, about 8 feet high, with rather small leaves, angular, downy branches, and long, loose, terminal panicles of small and greenish-white flowers. The leaves are wedge-shaped at the base, and when young have the lateral incisions split into a pair of unequal and very sharp teeth. Flowering in May and June. In the south and west of England it thrives best.

S. HYPERICIFOLIA (syn S. flagellata).--Asia Minor, 1640. A wiry twiggy shrub, fully 4 feet high, with entire leaves, and small, white flowers produced in umbels at the tips of the last year's shoots. It is a pretty and desirable species.

S. JAPONICA (syns S. callosa and *S. Fortunei*).--Japanese Spiraea. China and Japan, 1859. This is a robust species about a yard high, with large lanceolate leaves, and small, rosy-red flowers arranged in corymbose heads. Flowering at mid-summer. There are several fine varieties of this species, including S. japonica alba, a compact bush about a foot high with white flowers; S. japonica rubra differs from the type in having dark red flowers; S. japonica splendens, is a free-flowering dwarf plant, with peach-coloured flowers and suitable for forcing; and S. japonica superba, has dark rose-red flowers. S. Bumalda is a closely allied form, if not a mere variety of S. japonica. It is of dwarf habit, with dark reddish-purple flowers.

S. LAEVIGATA (syns S. altaicensis and *S. altaica*).--Smooth Spiraea. Siberia, 1774. A stout, spreading shrub about a yard high, with large, oblong-lanceolate, smooth, and stalkless leaves. The white flowers are arranged in racemose panicles, and produced in May.

S. LINDLEYANA.--Lindley's Spiraea. Himalayas. A handsome, tall-growing species, growing from 6 feet to 8 feet high, with very large pinnate leaves, and pretty white flowers in large terminal panicles. It is the largest-leaved Spiraea in cultivation, and forms a stately, handsome specimen, and produces its showy flowers in great quantities. Flowering at the end of summer.

S. MEDIA (syns S. confusa and *S. oblongifolia*).--Northern Asia, etc. The pure white flowers of this species are very freely produced in corymbs along the shoots of the previous season during the months of June and July. The lanceolate-elliptic leaves are serrate, or the smaller ones toothed near the apex only. Within the past few years the species has been brought into prominence for forcing purposes, for which it is admirably suited. It forms an upright, branching bush usually about 3 ft. high, and is best known under the name of S. confusa.

S. PRUNIFOLIA.--China and Japan, 1845. A twiggy-branched shrub growing 4 feet or 5 feet high, with oval, Plum-like leaves, and white flowers. There is a double-flowering variety named S. prunifolia flore-pleno, which is both distinct and beautiful.

S. ROTUNDIFOLIA.--Round-leaved Spiraea. Cashmere, 1839. A slender-branched shrub, having downy shoots, and round, blunt leaves, flowering in July.

S. SALICIFOLIA.--Willow-leaved Spiraea. Europe, and naturalised in Britain. An erect-growing, densely-branched shrub, with smooth shoots, which spring usually directly from the ground. Leaves large, lanceolate, smooth, doubly serrated, and produced plentifully. Flowers red or rose-coloured, and arranged in short, thyrsoid panicles. It flowers in July and August. S. salicifolia carnea has flesh-coloured flowers; S. salicifolia paniculata has white flowers; and S. salicifolia grandiflora has pink flowers as large again as the type. S. salicifolia alpestris (Mountain Spiraea) grows fully 2 feet high, with lanceolate, finely-toothed leaves, and loose, terminal panicles of pink or red flowers. From Siberia, and flowering in autumn. S. salicifolia latifolia (syn S. carpinifolia), the Hornbeam-leaved Spiraea, is a white-flowered variety, with leaves resembling those of the Hornbeam. From North America.

S. SORBIFOLIA.--Sorbus-leaved Spiraea. Siberia, 1759. A handsome, stout species, 4 feet high, with large, pinnate, bright green leaves, and small, white, sweetly-scented flowers produced in thyrsoid panicles.

S. THUNBERGII.--Thunberg's Spiraea. Japan. The white flowers of this species smell somewhat like those of the Hawthorn, and are freely produced on the leafless, twiggy stems, in March or early in April, according to the state of the weather. They are borne in axillary clusters from buds developed in the previous autumn, and are very welcome in spring, long before the others come into bloom. The bush varies from one to three feet high, and is clothed with linear-lanceolate, sharply serrated leaves.

S. TOMENTOSA.--Tomentose Spiraea. North America, 1736. This species grows 2 feet or 3 feet high, has rusty tomentose shoots and leaves, and large, dense, compound spikes of showy red flowers. Flowering in summer.

S. TRILOBATA (syn S. triloba).--Three-lobed Spiraea. Altaian Alps, 1801. This is a distinct species with horizontally arranged branches, small, roundish, three-lobed leaves, and white flowers arranged in umbel-like corymbs. It flowers in May, and is quite hardy.

S. UMBROSA (Shady Spiraea) and S. EXPANSA (Expanded-flowered Spiraea), the former from Northern India and the latter from Nepaul, are well suited for planting in somewhat shady situations, and are very ornamental species. The first mentioned grows about a foot high, with rather large leaves, and cymes of white flowers on long slender footstalks; while S. expansa has pink flowers, and lanceolate and coarsely serrated leaves.

There are other valuable-flowering kinds, such as S. capitata, with ovate leaves and white flowers; S. pikowiensis, a rare species with white flowers; S. cuneifolia, with wedge-shaped leaves and panicles of pretty white flowers; and S. vacciniaefolia, a dwarf-growing species, with small ovate, serrulated leaves, and showy, pure white flowers. S. betulifolia and S. chamaedrifolia flexuosa are worthy forms of free growth and bearing white flowers.

STAPHYLEA.

STAPHYLEA COLCHICA.--Colchican Bladder Nut. Caucasus. This is a very distinct shrub, about 6 feet high, with large clusters of showy white flowers. Being quite hardy, and very ornamental, this species is worthy the attention of planters.

S. PINNATA.--Job's Tears, or St. Anthony's Nut. South Europe. This is a straggling shrub, from 6 feet to 8 feet high, with white, racemose flowers, succeeded by bladder-like capsules.

S. TRIFOLIA.--North America, 1640. This is distinguished by its larger white flowers and trifoliolate leaves. It is the American Bladder Nut, but, like the latter, can hardly be included amongst ornamental plants.

All the Bladder Nuts grow freely in good light dampish loam.

STAUNTONIA.

STAUNTONIA HEXAPHYLLA.--China and Japan, 1876. This evergreen twining shrub is not to be generally recommended, it requiring wall protection even in southern England. The leaves are deep green and pinnate, while the greenish-white flowers are fragrant, and produced in the beginning of summer.

STUARTIA.

STUARTIA PENTAGYNA (syn Malachodendron ovatum).--North America, 1785. This differs only from the S. virginica in having five distinct styles, hence the name. Under very favourable circumstances this is the taller growing species, and the leaves and flowers are larger.

S. PSEUDO-CAMELLIA (syn S. grandiflora).--Japan, 1879. This is of recent introduction, and differs from the others in the flowers being rather larger, and of a purer white, and supplied with yellow instead of red stamens. It is quite hardy in Southern England and Ireland at least.

S. VIRGINICA (syn S. marylandica).--North America, 1743. This is a handsome free-growing shrub, of often 10 feet in height, with large, creamy-white flowers, that are rendered all the more conspicuous by the crimson-red stamens. The flowers--like those of a single Rose, and fully 2-1/2 inches across--are produced in May. Quite hardy, as many fine specimens in some of our old English gardens will point out.

Though, perhaps, rather exacting in their requirements, the Stuartias may be very successfully grown if planted in light, moist, peaty earth, and where they will be screened from cold, cutting winds.

STYRAX.

STYRAX AMERICANA and **S. PULVERULENTA** are not commonly cultivated, being far less showy than the Japanese species. They bear white flowers.

S. OFFICINALIS.--Storax. Levant, 1597. This is a small deciduous shrub, with ovate leaves, and short racemes of pretty pure white flowers. A not very hardy species, and only second-rate as an ornamental flowering shrub.

S. SERRULATA VIRGATA (syn S. japonica).--Japanese Storax. Japan. A neat-habited and dense-growing shrub, with pretty white flowers that are neatly set off by the showy yellow stamens. It is an extremely pretty shrub, with long, slender, much-branched shoots, furnished with ovate leaves, and deliciously-scented, snow-white bell-shaped flowers, produced for nearly the full length of the shoots. So far, this shrub of recent introduction has proved quite hardy. S. serrulata variegata is a well-marked and constant form.

SYMPHORICARPUS.

SYMPHORICARPUS OCCIDENTALIS.--Wolf Berry. North America. This species has larger and more freely-produced flowers, and smaller fruit than the
commonly-cultivated plant.

S. RACEMOSUS (syn Symphoria racemosus).--Snowberry. North America, 1817. One of the commonest shrubs in English gardens, with small, oval, entire leaves, and neat little racemes of pretty pink flowers, succeeded by the familiar snow-white berries, and for which the shrub is so remarkable.

S. VULGARIS.--Coral Berry, Common St. Peter's Wort. North America, 1730. This is readily distinguished by its showy and freely-produced coral berries. There is a very neat and much sought after variety, having conspicuous green and yellow leaves, and named S. vulgaris foliis variegatis.

The Snowberries are of no great value as ornamental shrubs, but owing to their succeeding well in the very poorest and stoniest of soils, and beneath the shade and drip of trees, it is to be recommended that they are not lost sight of. They grow and spread freely, and are therefore useful where unchecked and rampant shrub growth is desirable.

SYMPLOCOS.

SYMPLOCOS JAPONICA (syn S. lucida).--A small growing and not very desirable species from Japan (1850).

S. TINCTORIA.--Sweet-leaf, or Horse Sugar. South United States, 1780. This is a small-growing shrub, with clusters of fragrant yellow flowers, but it is not very hardy unless planted against a sheltered and sunny wall.

SYRINGA.

SYRINGA CHINENSIS (syns. S. dubia and **S. rothomagensis**).--Rouen, or Chinese Lilac. A plant of small growth, with narrow leaves, and reddish-violet flowers. It is said to have been raised by M. Varin, of the Botanic Garden, Rouen, as a hybrid between S. vulgaris and S. persica, 1795.

S. EMODI.--Himalayas, 1840. This is a desirable species, that forms a stout bush or small tree, with oblong, reticulately-veined leaves, and erect, dense panicles of white flowers, that are sometimes lilac tinged. The flowers are strongly scented, and borne in great profusion late in the season. There is a variegated form, S. Emodi variegata, and another named S. Emodi villosa, both good varieties.

S. JAPONICA (syns S. amurensis and **Ligustrina amurensis**).--Japan. This is of recent introduction, and is a decided acquisition, producing in summer large and dense clusters of creamy-white flowers. It is a very desirable species, and though coming from Japan seems to be perfectly hardy.

S. JOSIKAEA, Josika's Lilac, is of Hungarian origin (1835), and is so totally different from the others as to be well worthy of special attention. It rarely exceeds 6 feet in height, with dark-green, wrinkled leaves, and erect spikes of pale mauve flowers.

S. PERSICA (Persian Lilac).--Persia, 1640. This is a distinct small-growing species, with slender, straight branches, and lilac or white flowers produced in small clusters. The form bearing white flowers is named S. persica alba; and there is one with neatly divided foliage called S. persica laciniata.

S. VULGARIS.--Common Lilac, or Pipe Tree. Persia and Hungary, 1597. This is one of the commonest and most highly praised of English garden shrubs, and one that has given rise, either by natural variation or by crossing with other species, to a great number of superior forms. The following include the best and most ornamental of the numerous varieties:--alba, pure white flowers; alba-grandiflora, very large clusters of white flowers; alba-magna, and alba virginalis, both good white-flowering forms; Dr. Lindley, large clusters of reddish-lilac flowers; Charles X., purplish-lilac flowers, but white when forced; Souvenir De Ludwig Spath, with massive clusters of richly coloured flowers; Glorie de Moulins, Marie Legrange, Noisetteana, Duchesse de Nemours, and Vallettiana, all beautiful flowering forms that are well worthy of cultivation, and that are of the simplest growth.

The double-flowered varieties, for which we are much indebted to M. Victor Lemoine, of Nancy, are fast gaining favour with cultivators in this country, and rightly, too, for they include several very handsome, full flowered forms. The following are best known:--

S. vulgaris Alphonse Lavallee, with full double red flowers, changing to mauve.

" Emile Lemoine, mauve-pink, suffused with white; very handsome.

" La Tour d'Auvergne, mauve shaded with rose. A beautiful and very dark coloured form.

" Lemoinei, nearly resembling our common species, but with full double flowers.

" Leon Simon, light pink, mauve shaded.

" Madame Lemoine, the finest form, bearing very large pure white double flowers.

" Michael Buchner, rosy lilac.

" VirginitE, whitish pink, nearly white when fully expanded.

President Grevy is one of the same beautiful group. The blooms are large, double, and produced in very massive clusters, and of a light bluish-lilac tint, when forced almost white. The first of this group, S. vulgaris Lemoinei, was sent out about 1884, and was then awarded a certificate by the R.H.S. The range in colouring of these Lilacs is rather confined, so that the various forms resemble one another in no small degree, particularly when the flowers are opened under glass. From the large size of the flower bunches, and the individual flowers being double, they are all of great beauty, and being quite hardy still further enhances their value for outdoor gardening purposes.

The Lilacs grow freely in any soil of fair quality, but a free, rich, and not too dry loam, would seem to suit the majority of these plants best.

TAMARIX.

TAMARIX GALLICA.--Common Tamarisk. India to Europe. This shrub often in favoured maritime places reaches to a height of fully 10 feet, with long and slender branches, and spikes of pretty, rosy-pink flowers produced at the end of summer. For sea-side planting, it is an invaluable shrub, and on account of its feathery appearance and wealth of showy flowers is well worthy of being included in our list of ornamental and useful shrubs.

T. PARVIFLORA (syns T. africana and *T. tetrandra*), South-eastern Europe and Levant, is a nearly allied species, with white, pinky-tinged flowers.

TECOMA.

TECOMA GRANDIFLORA (syn Bignonia grandiflora), from China and Japan (1800), is not so hardy as T. radicans, although in certain maritime districts it succeeds fairly well. The flowers are very attractive, being of a rich orange-scarlet, and produced in drooping clusters. Both foliage and flowers are larger than those of T. radicans. It wants a warm, sunny wall, and light, rich, and well-drained soil, and if only for its lovely flowers, it is well worthy of coddling and good treatment.

T. RADICANS (syn Bignonia radicans).--Trumpet Flower. North America, 1640. An old occupant of our gardens and one of the most beautiful wall plants in cultivation. It is a tall climber, of sometimes fully 20 feet in height, with graceful pinnate leaves, and handsome trumpet-shaped scarlet-red flowers, that are at their best about mid-summer, though the period of flowering extends over a considerable length of time. The stems are long, twisted, and wiry, and like those of the Ivy send out roots at the joints and so fasten the plant in position. Few climbing plants are more attractive than the Trumpet Flower, and being hardy in most parts of the country, and free of growth, is to be recommended for covering walls, and arches, or similar structures. T. radicans major is of more robust growth than the species, with larger foliage and paler flowers. The orange-scarlet flowers are produced in terminal corymbs.

TILIA.

TILIA VULGARIS (syns T. europea and *T. intermedia*).--Lime, or Linden Tree. Europe, Caucasus, and naturalised in Britain. Probably none of the Limes would be included in a list of ornamental-flowering trees and shrubs, still that they are of great interest and beauty even in that state cannot be denied. The common species as well as its numerous varieties have sweetly scented, yellowish-white flowers in terminal cymes, and are, though individually small, highly ornamental when fully developed. Other species of great interest when in flower are T. alba (syn T. argentea), Silver Lime; T. petiolaris, a curious and beautiful species; and T. euchlora.

The various species and varieties of Lime succeed well in almost any class of soil, but rich loam on sand is considered the most suitable for their perfect development.

ULEX.

ULEX EUROPAEUS.--Furze, Gorse, or Whin. This pretty native shrub needs no description, suffice it to say that it is one of the handsomest-flowering shrubs in cultivation. U. europaeus flore-pleno (Double-flowered Gorse) is even more beautiful than the species, the wealth of golden flowers almost hiding the plant from view. U. europaeus strictus (Irish Furze) is of more erect and slender growth, and less rigid than the common species.

U. NANUS.---Dwarf Gorse, Cat Whin, and Tam Furze. This differs considerably from the common plant, not only in stature, but in the time of flowering. In this species the bracts at the calyx base are small compared with those of U. europaeus, while the smaller flowers are produced during summer, and when not a bloom is to be found on its supposed parent. It is of dense growth, the tallest stems rarely rising from the ground to a greater height than about 15 inches.

All the Furze family succeed admirably in the poorest of soil; indeed, a dry gravelly bank would seem to be their favourite haunt.

VACCINIUM.

VACCINIUM CORYMBOSUM.--Canada to Carolina and Georgia, 1765. This is one of the most beautiful and showy species, with dense clusters of small, pinky flowers.

V. MYRTILLUS.--Whortleberry, Bilberry, Blackberry, and Blueberry. A native plant, with angular stems, ovate-toothed leaves, and pinky-white flowers, succeeded by bright, bluish-black berries.

V. PENNSYLVANICUM.--New England to Virginia, 1772. This has rather inconspicuous flowers, and is of greatest value for the autumnal foliage tints.

V. VITIS-IDEA (Cowberry, Flowering Box, or Brawlins) a native species, has racemose flowers, and red berries.

Other species that might be included are V. canadense, V. stamineum, V. frondosum, and V. ligustrifolium.

The various species of Vaccinium are of dwarf or procumbent growth, and only suitable for planting in beds, or on rockwork, where they will not be lost sight of. They thrive best in soil of a peaty nature.

VERONICA.

VERONICA PINQUIFOLIA.--New Zealand, 1870. This is one of the hardiest species, but it is of low growth, and only suitable for alpine gardening. It is a dwarf spreading shrub, with intensely glaucous leaves and white flowers.

V. TRAVERSII.--New Zealand, 1873. This may be considered as one of the few species of hardy Veronicas. It grows about 4 feet high, with deep green leaves arranged in rows, and white flowers, produced late in summer. It is a very free-growing shrub, of perfect hardihood, and one of, if not the best for general planting.

The above two species are, so far as is at present known, the hardiest in cultivation, although there are many kinds that will succeed well under very favourable conditions, and particularly when planted by the sea-side. Other half-hardy species might include V. salicifolia (Willow-leaved Veronica), with long, narrow leaves, and white or purplish flowers; V. ligustrifolia (Privet-leaved Veronica), with spikes of feathery-white flowers; V. speciosa, with erect spikes of purplish-blue flowers; and V. Andersoni, a hybrid form, with spikes of bluish-violet flowers.

The dwarf or alpine species might include V. cupressoides, with Cypress-like foliage, V. Lyallii, V. carnosula, and others, but such hardly come within our scope.

VIBURNUM.

VIBURNUM ACERIFOLIUM.--Dockmackie. New England to Carolina, 1736. This is one of the handsomest members of the family, being of slender growth and compact and neat in habit. It grows to fully 4 feet in height, and is well supplied with neatly three-lobed leaves, these in the autumn turning to a deep crimson. The flowers, too, are highly ornamental, being borne in fair sized clusters, and white or yellowish-white. It is a very desirable and beautiful plant, quite hardy, and of free growth in any fairly rich soil.

V. AWAFUKII.--Japan, 1842. This is another rare and beautiful plant, of neat habit, and producing an abundance of showy white flowers, that are, however, seldom produced in this country.

V. DAHURICUM.--Dahuria, 1785. This is a charming hardy species, which in May and June is covered with numerous umbels of showy white flowers. It forms a rather spreading bush of 6 feet or 8 feet high, with gray downy branches, and neat foliage. The berries are oval-oblong, red at first, but becoming black and faintly scented when fully ripe.

V. DENTATUM.--Arrowwood. A native of the United States, 1763. This can be recommended as a distinct and beautiful shrub, with cymes of white flowers that are produced in plenty. The leaves are dark green, smooth, and shining, and strongly veined, while the bark is ash-coloured, and the berries bright blue.

V. LANTANA.--Wayfaring Tree. Europe (Britain). This is a native species of large bush, or almost tree growth, with rugose, oblong, serrulated leaves, and large, flat cymes of white flowers appearing in May and June. The whole tree is usually covered with a scaly tomentum, while the fruit is a black flattened drupe.

V. LENTAGO.--Sheepberry and Sweet Viburnum. North America, 1761. This resembles our native V. Lantana, with dense clusters of white blossoms succeeded by black berries.

V. MACROCEPHALUM (syn V. Fortunei).--China, 1844. This is a Chinese species, but one that cannot be depended on as hardy enough to withstand our most severe winters. It has very large heads or panicles of white neutral flowers. Against a sunny wall and in a cosy nook it may occasionally be found doing fairly well, but it is not to be generally recommended.

V. NUDUM.--American Withe Rod. Canada to Georgia, 1752. This is also worthy of being included in a selection of these shrubs.

V. OPULUS.--Guelder Rose. A native shrub of great beauty, whether in foliage, flower, or fruit. The leaves are variously lobed or deeply toothed, large and handsome, and the flower heads of good size, flat, and composed of a number of small flowers, the outer only being sterile. Individually the flowers are dull and inconspicuous, but being produced in amazing quantity, they have a very pleasing and effective appearance. The great bunches of clear pinky berries render a fair-sized plant particularly handsome and attractive, and for which alone, as also beauty of autumnal foliage, the shrub is well worthy of extensive culture. It grows fully 15 feet high, and may frequently be seen as much through. V. Opulus sterilis (Snowball Tree) is one of the commonest occupants of our shrubberies, and a decidedly ornamental-flowering shrub. The large, almost globular flower heads hanging from every branch tip, are too well-known to require description, and have made the shrub one of the most popular in ornamental planting.

V. PAUCIFLORUM is a native of cold, moist woods from Labrador to Alaska, and may best be described as a miniature V. Opulus. It rarely grows more than 4 feet high, with small cymes of flowers, that are devoid of the neutral flowers of that species.

V. PLICATUM, from Japan 1846, is another very beautiful and desirable shrub, of rather dwarf, spreading growth, and having the leaves deeply wrinkled, plaited, and serrated on the margins. The flowers resemble those of the commonly cultivated species, but they are rather larger, and of a purer white. It is a decidedly ornamental species of easy growth in any good soil, and where not exposed to cold winds.

V. PRUNIFOLIUM, New England to Carolina, 1731, with Plum-like leaves, and pretty white flowers, is another free-growing and beautiful North American species.

V. PYRIFOLIUM.--Pear-leaved Viburnum. Pennsylvania to New Jersey, 1812. This is a rarely-seen, but very ornamental species, with oval-shaped, finely-toothed leaves, that are borne on short, slightly-winged stalks about half-an-inch long. Flowers sweetly scented, white, and in broad corymbs, the feathery appearance of the long, projecting stamens, each tipped with a golden anther, adding considerably to the beauty of the flowers.

V. RETICULATUM and V. LAEVIGATUM are rarely seen species, but of interest botanically, if not for floral beauty.

V. TINUS.--Laurustinus. South Europe, 1596. So commonly cultivated a shrub needs no description here, sufficient to say that the handsome evergreen foliage and pretty pinky-white flowers assign to it a first position amongst hardy ornamental flowering shrubs, V. Tinus strictum has darker foliage than the species, is more upright, rather more hardy, but not so profuse in the bearing of flowers. V. Tinus lucidum (Glossy-leaved Laurustinus), of the several varieties of Laurustinus has the largest foliage, finest flowers, and altogether is of the most robust growth. It is, unfortunately, not very hardy, probably in that respect not even equalling the parent plant. Usually it does not flower freely, neither are the flowers produced so early as in the species, but individually they are much larger. It is of tall growth, and rarely forms the neat, dense bush, for which the common shrub is so admired. V. Tinus rotundifolium has rounded leaves; and V. Tinus rotundifolium variegatum has irregularly variegated leaves.

VINCA.

VINCA MAJOR.--Band-plant, Cut-finger, and Larger Periwinkle. Europe (Britain). For trailing over tree-stumps or rockwork this pretty evergreen shrub has a distinctive value, the bright green leaves and showy deep blue flowers rendering it both conspicuous and ornamental. V. major elegantissima is a decided variety, the leaves being neatly and evenly variegated, and making the plant of great value for bank or rock-work decoration.

V. MINOR.--Lesser Periwinkle. This is of much smaller growth than the preceding, and differs, too, in not having the leaf-margins ciliated. The variety V. minor flore-albo has white flowers, those of the normal plant being pale blue; V. minor flore-pleno differs in having double blue flowers; V. minor foliis aureis has golden-tinted leaves; and V. minor foliis argenteis bears silvery mottled and very attractive foliage.

They are all of simple growth, succeeding well in somewhat shady situations, and in by no means the richest of soil. As they run about freely and soon cover an extent of ground they are rendered of great value for a variety of purposes.

VITEX.

VITEX AGNUS-CASTUS.--Chaste Tree, Hemp Tree, and Monk's Pepper-tree. A South European shrub (1670), growing from 6 feet to 10 feet high, with digitate leaves that are almost hoary beneath, and spikes of small violet flowers. It is not very hardy, although in some of the warmer parts of southern England and Ireland, fair-sized, healthy-looking specimens are now and then to be met with. As a wall plant, however, it succeeds best, and for which purpose, with its neat foliage and pretty flowers, it is peculiarly suitable.

VITIS.

VITIS HETEROPHYLLA HUMILIFOLIA.--Turquoise-berried Vine. North China and Japan, 1868. The leaves of this Vine are three to five lobed, and the small flowers freely produced in slightly branching cymes. The latter are succeeded by their most interesting and attractive berries, that ripen in September and October. They are pale china-blue, marked all over with very dark specks. The stems grow to a height of 4 feet to 8 feet, and should be trained against a wall in a sunny position to ripen the berries. The plant is perfectly hardy. The variety V. heterophylla variegata is a dwarf, low-growing plant with variegated leaves, and is used for pot work, for covering the ground in sub-tropical bedding designs, and might be used to great advantage for rambling over large stones in the rock garden.

WISTARIA.

WISTARIA CHINENSIS (syns W. sinensis, Glycine chinensis, and *G. sinensis*).--Chinese Wistaria. China, 1816. This is the only species at all common in gardens, and by far the handsomest in cultivation. It justly ranks amongst the most beautiful of hardy climbing shrubs, and is invaluable as a wall plant, or for clothing the bare stems of sparsely foliaged trees. The purplish-lilac flowers are produced in long, drooping racemes in early summer. W. chinensis alba has pretty white flowers; W. chinensis flore-pleno has not proved very satisfactory, but when seen at its best, which is, however, but rarely, the double flowers are both beautiful and showy; W. chinensis variegata has badly variegated foliage; and W. chinensis macrobotrys is a plant of great beauty with very long racemes of pale lavender flowers, but they vary a good deal in colour, those of some plants being almost white. It is a very desirable variety, and one that when better known is sure to attract attention.

W. FRUTESCENS (syns Glycine frutescens and *Thyrsanthus frutescens*).--North America, 1724. This is a very handsome deciduous climbing species from North America. The flowers, which appear towards autumn, are bluish purple and fragrant, and borne in erect racemes. It is quite hardy and equally suitable with the Chinese species for using as a wall covering. W. frutescens magnifica is an improved form of the species.

W. JAPONICA.--Japan. A bush-like species bearing white flowers, but it is rarely seen in cultivation. It is, however, quite hardy, and succeeds well in the bush state at Kew.

W. MULTIJUGA.--Japan, 1874. Resembles somewhat our commonly-cultivated species, and has pale purple flowers arranged in long racemes. It is a very ornamental and desirable species, but the flowers are not borne in great quantity.

The Wistarias are of simple culture, but succeed best in rather rich alluvial soil, and where protection from cold winds is provided.

XANTHOCERAS.

XANTHOCERAS SORBIFOLIA.--China, 1870. An extremely pretty flowered and handsome leaved shrub, but owing to its late introduction is not yet well known. So far it has proved itself perfectly hardy in this country, there being specimens at wide distances apart that have stood uninjured through our past severe winters.

The leaves are pale green, and pinnate, somewhat resembling those of the Rowan Tree. Flowers five petalled, creamy white, sometimes very slightly tinged with flesh colour, with a coppery red or violet-purple centre, and disposed in racemes. When fully expanded they are an inch across, and somewhat reflexed. It flowers early in April, with the appearance of the leaves, the blooms being produced in great abundance, in spike-like clusters fully seven inches long, and succeeded by a small green Pear-like fruit. This is one of the most distinct and handsome of recently introduced shrubs, and will, when more widely disseminated, be largely planted for purely ornamental purposes. It grows from 10 feet to about 15 feet high.

XANTHORHIZA.

XANTHORHIZA APIIFOLIA.--Yellow-root. Pennsylvania, 1776. A small growing shrub, with yellow creeping roots, from which suckers are thrown up profusely. The leaves are irregularly pinnate, and the minute flowers, which are borne in large, branching spikes, are of a peculiar dark purple colour. It prefers a cool, moist situation.

YUCCA.

YUCCA FILAMENTOSA.--Silk Grass. North America, 1675. A well-known and beautiful plant, with numerous leaves arranged in a dense rosette, and from 1 foot to 2 feet long by 2 inches broad. Flower scape rising to 5 feet or 6 feet in height, and bearing numerous flowers that are each about 2 inches deep. There is a beautiful variegated form of this species named Y. filamentosa variegata, and one with much narrower leaves than the typical species, and known as Y. filamentosa angustifolia.

Y. GLORIOSA.--The Mound Lily. United States, 1596. This is another well-known hardy species, with long, sharp-pointed leaves, and a handsome, much branched scape, of flowers that are each about 2 inches deep. There are several varieties, differing in colour of foliage, including Y. gloriosa glaucescens, with decidedly glaucous foliage; Y. gloriosa superba, with rigid leaves and a shorter and denser flower scape; and another with variegated leaves. Y. gloriosa recurvifolia is usually dwarfer in the stem than the type, and more inclined to branch than the other species, and less rigid, with recurving leaves that are not so sharp-pointed, The flower panicle is large and very much branched.

The Yuccas all do well if planted in light loam of good quality.

ZELKOVA.

ZELKOVA ACUMINATA (syns Z. japonica and **Planera acuminata**).--Japan. This resembles very nearly our common Elm in appearance, and being perfectly hardy is to be recommended for planting in this country.

Z. CRENATA (syns Planera crenata and **P. Richardi**).--Zelkova Tree. Western Asia to Mount Caucasus, 1760. This is a handsome, large growing tree, with oblong deeply-crenated leaves, and small and inconspicuous flowers. For avenue planting or as a standard specimen this is a valuable tree, being quite hardy, and of free and quick growth. P. crenata pendula is a good weeping form, and worthy of culture.

Z. CRETICA.--Crete. A pretty small growing bush or tree of about 20 feet in height, with crenate, leathery, dark green leaves, which are usually fully an inch in length. The leaves are hairy, and the twigs, too, are thickly covered with short grey hairs.

ZAUSCHNERIA.

ZAUSCHNERIA CALIFORNICA.--Californian Fuchsia, or Humming Birds' Trumpet. California and Mexico, 1847. A small-growing, densely-branched shrub, with linear-lanceolate silvery pubescent leaves, and bright red or scarlet tubular flowers, with a long, slender style resembling some of the Fuchsias. It is a pretty and distinct Alpine shrub, and not being perfectly hardy should be assigned a rather warm and sheltered position.

ZENOBIA.

ZENOBIA SPECIOSA (syn Andromeda speciosa and **A. cassinaefolia**).--South United States, 1800. This is a distinct and pretty hardy species, a native of swampy low-lying districts. It grows about four feet high, and bears pure white, bell-shaped, Lily-of-the-Valley like flowers in great abundance during the summer. In too dry situations it becomes sparse of foliage and unhappy, but grows and flowers freely in light, peaty soil. Z. speciosa pulverulenta is a very desirable variety, the whole plant, stems, foliage, and flowers, being of a pleasing light gray or white colour. Individually the flowers are larger than those of the species.

ADDENDA.

EXOCHORDA.

EXOCHORDA GRANDIFLORA (syn Spiraea grandiflora).--North China. This handsome shrub forms a much branched, spreading bush, about 4 feet to 6 feet high, and flowers abundantly in May. The habit is similar to that of a shrubby Spiraea, but the pure white flowers are as large as those of some of the species of Cherry, and quite unlike those of any known species of Spiraea. The flowers are liable to injury sometimes from late spring frosts, but the plant itself is quite hardy. As a bush on the lawn it is nevertheless highly ornamental and desirable.

MYRICARIA.

MYRICARIA GERMANICA.--Europe, Asia, 1582. A tall, somewhat straggling shrub, very similar to the Tamarisk, with terminal spikes of pink or rosy flowers, produced freely nearly all the summer. It succeeds well in this country in sea-side situations, and is often described as a Tamarisk by gardeners.

TREES SUITABLE FOR PLANTING IN TOWNS.

Acer macrophylla

saccharinum
Aesculus Hippocastanum
  rubicunda
Ailanthus glandulosa
Crataegus Oxyacantha
  flore-plena
  tenacetifolia
Catalpa bignonioides
Cerasus (Prunus), nearly all
Gleditschia triacanthos
Liriodendron tulipiiera
Magnolia acuminata
  glauca
Pyrus of sorts
Robinia Pseud-acacia and its varieties
  viscosa
Sophora japonica
Tilia, in variet.

SHRUBS FOR TOWN PLANTING.

Amelanchier, in variety
Arbutus Unedo
Berberis Aquifolium
  vulgaris
Cistus ladaniferus
  laurifolius
Colutea arborescens
Daphne Laureola
  Mezereum
  pontica
Deutzia crenata

gracilis
Forsythia suspensa
  viridissima
Griselinia littoralis
Hibiscus syriacus
Hypericum calycinum
Hypericum nepalense
Koelrenteria paniculata
Leycesteria formosa
Philadelphus Gordonianus
Prunus nana
Pyrus japonica
Rhus Cotinus
Ribes aureum
  sanguineum
Skimmia japonica
Syringa (nearly all)
Ulex europaeus fl.-pl.
Viburnum Opulus
Weigelia rosea
Yucca gloriosa
  recurva

TREES FOR THE SEASIDE.

Acer campestre
  saccharinum
Arbutus Unedo
Ailanthus glandulosa
Aesculus Hippocastanum
  rubicunda
Catalpa bignonioides

Fraxinus Ornus

SHRUBS FOR THE SEASIDE.

Atriplex halimus
Cerasus lusitanica
Cytisus Laburnum
  scoparius
Euonymus japonicus
  europaeus
Fabiana imbricata
Griselinia littoralis
Hippophae rhomnoides
Ilex Aquifolium
Laurus nobilis
Lycium europaeum
Prunus Padus
Rhamnus frangula
Ribes sanguineum
Rosa spinosissima
Shepherdia argentea
Spirea adiantifolia
Syringa persica
  vulgaris
Symphoricarpus racemosus
Tamarix gallica
  germanica
Ulex europaea
Viburnum Tinus

THE FLOWERING SEASONS OF TREES AND SHRUBS.

The asterisk * after the name denotes that the species continues in flower for a longer period than the month under which it is placed.

JANUARY.

Erica carnea*
Chimonanthus fragrans*
Crataegus Oxyacantha praecox*
Jasminum nudiflorum*
Ulex europaeus*
Viburnum Tinus*

FEBRUARY.

Cornus Mas*
Daphne Laureola*
  Mezereum*
Hamamelis japonica
Lonicera fragrantissima*
Magnolia conspicua*
Parrotia persica*
Pittosporum Tobira*
Prunus nana*
  Davidiana*
Rosmarinus officinalis*

MARCH.

Arbutus Andrachne*
Berberis japonica*
Erica mediterranea*
Forsythia viridissima*

Garrya elliptica
Magnolia stellata*
Nuttallia cerasiformis*
Prunus Amygdalus*
  ilicifolia*
  japonica*
  spinosa*
  triloba*
  tomentosa
Rhododendron dahuricum
  ledifolium
Skimmia Fortunei
Spiraea Thunbergi*
Xanthoriza apiifolia*

APRIL.

Akebia quinata*
Amelanchier alnifolia
  canadensis
  vulgaris
Berberis Aquifolium*
  Darwinii*
  pinnata
  vulgaris
Caesalpinia sepiaria
Caragana frutescens
  spinosa*
Ceanothus cuneatus*
  rigidus*
Clematis cirrhosa*
  florida*
Cornus florida

Cytisus scoparius*
Daphne altaica
  Blagayana
  Cneorum*
  Genkwa
  sericea
Deutzia gracilis*
Diervilla rosea*
Drimys aromatica
Fothergilla alnifolia*
Fremontia californica
Halesia diptera
  tetraptera
Kalmia glauca*
Laburnum vulgare*
Ledum latifolium
  palustre
Lonicera Caprifolium*
  tatarica*
Magnolia cordata*
  Fraseri
  Lennei
  obovata discolor
Pieris floribunda*
  japonica*
Prunus Avium Juliana
  cerasifera
  cerasifera Pissardii
  Cerasus
  domestica
  divaricata
  Mahaleb
  maritima

Hardy Ornamental Flowering Trees and Shrubs

  Padus*
  paniculata flore-pleno
  Puddum*
  sinensis
Pyrus angustifolia
  baccata*
  floribunda*
  japonica Maulei
Pyrus prunifolia*
  rivularis*
  sinica
  vestita
Rhododendron campanulatum
  Rhodora*
Rhodotypos kerrioides
Ribes aureum*
  cereum
  floridum*
  sanguineum
Rosa indica*
Sambucus racemosa*
Skimmia japonica
  Laureola
Spiraea prunifolia
Stuartia virginica*
Syringa Emodi
Xanthoceras sorbifolia

MAY.

Abelia triflora*
Aesculus glabra
  Hippocastanum

Arbutus Menziesii
Berberis aristata*
 Bealei
 empetrifolia
 sinensis
 trifoliolata
 Wallichiana
Calycanthus floridus*
Caragana arborescens
 microphylla
Ceanothus dentatus*
Cercis canadensis
 Siliquastrum
Chionanthus retusa
 virginica
Citrus trifoliata
Cladrastis tinctoria
Clematis alpina*
 montana*
Cornus canadensis
 stolonifera
Coronilla Emerus*
Crataegus Azarolus
 Azarolus Aronia
 coccinea
 cordata*
 Crus-galli
 Douglasii
 Oxyacantha*
 parvifolia
 Pyracantha
 tenacetifolia
Cytisus albus*

albus incarnate*
 biflorus*
Daphne alpina*
Deutzia crenata*
Epigaea repens
Fabiana imbricata
Fraxinus Ornus*
 Mariesii
Gaultheria Shallon
Genista lusitanica
 pilosa*
 prostrata*
Halesia parviflora
Halimodendron argenteum*
Laburnum Adami*
Leiophyllum buxifolium*
 Leucothoe axillaris
 Catesbaei
Magnolia acuminata*
 glauca
 Umbrella
Ostrya carpinifolia
Paeonia Moutan
Pernettya mucronata*
Philadelphus coronarius
Pieris Mariana*
 ovalifolia
Piptanthus nepalensis
Polygala Chamaebuxus*
Prunus Chamaecerasus
 pennsylvanica
 virginiana*
Pyrus Aria*

   Aucuparia*
   coronaria
   germanica
   prunifolia
   sinensis
   Smithii*
   torminalis
Rhododendron arborescens
  calendulaceum
  Collettiana
  ferrugineum*
  flavum
  hirsutum*
  molle
  ponticum
  racemosum
Ribes speciosum
Robinia hispida
  Pseud-Acacia*
  viscosa
Rosa spinosissima*
Rubus biflorus
  deliciosus
  spectabilis
Sophora tetraptera
Spiraea cantoniensis
  laevigata
  trilobata
Staphylea pinnata*
  trifolia*
Stuartia pentagyna*
Syringa chinensis*
  Josikaea

persica*
 vulgaris*
Vaccinium corymbosum*
 pennsylvanicum
Viburnum acerifolium*
 Lantana*
 Lentago*
 nudum*
 plicatum*
 prunifolium
 pyrifolium*
Wistaria chinensis*
 multijuga*
Exochorda grandiflora

JUNE.

Adenocarpus decorticans*
Aesculus californica*
Andromeda polifolia
Bryanthus erectus
Buddleia globosa*
 Lindleyana*
 paniculata*
Calophaca wolgarica*
Calycanthus occidentalis*
Carpenteria californica
Castanea saliva
Catalpa speciosa
Ceanothus azureus*
Choisya ternata*
Cistus crispus*
 ladaniferus

    laurifolius*
    monspeliensis*
    purpureus*
    salvifolius*
Clematis lanuginosa*
    patens*
    Viorna
    Viticella
Colutea arborescens*
    cruenta*
Cornus circinata
    macrophylla
Crataegus nigra*
Cytisus decumbens
    nigricans
Daboecia polifolia
Diervilla floribunda*
    grandiflora*
Escallonia macrantha*
Fuchsia Riccartoni*
Genista aetnensis*
    saggitalis
Helianthemum halimifolium*
    lasianthum
    lavendulaefolium*
Helianthemum pilosum*
    polifolium*
    umbellatum*
Hypericum calycinum*
    patulum*
Itea virginica
Jamesia americana
Jasminum revolutum*

Kalmia angustifolia
  latifolia*
Kerria japonica*
Laburnum alpinum
  caramanicum
Ligustrum japonicum
  lucidum*
  ovalitolium*
  sinense*
Liriodendron tulipifera*
Lyonia paniculata
Magnolia macrophylla
Myricaria germanica*
Myrtus communis*
Neillia opulifolia
Olearia macrodonta
Oxydendrum arboreum*
Philadelphus grandiflorus
  hirsutus
  inodorus
  Lewisi
  microphyllus*
Phlomis fruticosa
Plagianthus pulchellus*
Potentilla fruticosa
Prunus lusitanica
Rhododendron californicum
  campylocarpum
  chrysanthum
Rhus Cotinus*
Robinia dubia*
Rosa alba*
  centifolia*

damascena*
gallica*
lutea
rubiginosa
rugosa
sempervirens*
Rubus arcticus
laciniatus*
odoratus*
Sambucus nigra
Spiraea bullata*
cana*
chamaedrifolia*
decumbens*
hypericifolia*
japonica*
media*
Staphylea colchica
Stuartia Pseudo-Camellia*
Syringa japonica*
Tecoma radicans*
Tilia vulgaris*
Veronica pinquifolia
Traversii*
Viburnum dahuricum*
dentatum
macrocephalum
Opulus*
Yucca filamentosa
Zenobia speciosa*

JULY.

Aesculus parviflora*
Berberis Fortunei
Ceanothus americanus*
Clematis Flammula*
　Vitalba*
Cornus alba
　alternifolia
　tartarica
Escallonia floribunda
　Phillipiana*
　pterocladon
　rubra*
Eucryphia pinnatifolia*
Fuchsia macrostema globosa*
Genista anxanctica*
　cinerea
　germanica
　hispanica*
　radiata*
　tinctoria*
Gordonia lasianthus*
Hydrangea hortensis*
Hypericum elatum
　fasciculatum
　hircinum*
　prolificum*
　uralum*
Jasminum fruticans*
　humile*
Kalmia hirsuta*
Ligustrum Ibota*

   Quihoi*
Lonicera Xylosteum*
Periploca graeca*
Philadelphus Gordonianus
  satzumi
Photinia arbutifolia
Plagianthus Lyalli
Philadelphus Lemoinei
Rhododendron catawbiense
  maximum
  viscosum
Rosa bracteata
  hemisphaerica
Spartium junceum*
Spiraea bella*
  discolor ariaefolia
Spiraea salicifolia*
  sorbifolia*
  tomentosa
Tamarix gallica*
  parviflora*
Tilia petiolaris*
Wistaria japonica*
Yucca gloriosa
Zauschneria californica

AUGUST.

Abelia chinensis*
Calluna vulgaris*
Catalpa bignonioides
Clerodendron foetidum
Erica cinerea*

Escallonia illinita
Gordonia pubescens
Hedysarum multijugum
Hibiscus syriacus*
Hypericum oblongifolium
Leycesteria formosa*
Loropetalum chinense*
Magnolia grandiflora*
Nesaea salicifolia*
Passiflora caerulea*
Rubus nutkanus
Sophora japonica*
Spiraea Douglasii
  Lindleyana
Vitex Agnus-castus

SEPTEMBER.

Arbutus Unedo*
Baccharis halimifolia
Clerodendron trichotomum
Clethra acuminata*
  alnifolia
Daphne Cneorum*
Hydrangea paniculata grandiflora*
Olearia Haastii
  Gunniana
Photinia japonica
Microglossa albescens*
Tecoma grandiflora*

OCTOBER.

Berberidopsis corallina
Berberris nervosa*
Caryopteris Mastacanthus
Hamamelis virginica*
Lespedeza bicolor

NOVEMBER.

Azara microphylla
Cassinia fulvida
Chimonanthus fragrans*
Jasminum nudiflorum*

DECEMBER.

Chimonanthus fragrans*
Lardizabala biternata
Viburnum Tinus*

INDEX.

Synonymous names are printed in italics.

Aaron's Beard,
Abelia chinensis,
  rupestris,
  triflora,
Adenocarpus **Boissieri**,
  decorticans,
Aesculus californica,
  chinensis,
  flava,
  flava discolor,
  glabra,
  Hippocastanum,
  Pavia,
  Pavia atrosanguinea,
  Pavia humilis,
  Pavia macrocarpa,
  Pavia Whitleyana,
  parviflora,
  rubicunda,
Ailanthus *flavescens*,
  glandulosa,
Akebia quinata,

Alabama Snow Wreath,
Alder, the berry bearing
Alexandrian Laurel,
Almond, AbbE David's
　common,
Aloysia citriodora,
Aloysia. See Lippia
Alpine Rose,
Althaea frutex,
Amelanchier alnifolia,
　canadensis,
　vulgaris,
American Great Laurel,
American Withe Rod,
Ammyrsine buxifoiia,
Amoor Yellow Wood,
Amorpha canescens,
　fruticosa,
Amygdatus communis,
　dulcis,
　Besseriana,
　Boissieri,
　Lindleyi,
　nana,
　persica flore-pleno,
Amygdalus. See Prunus,
Andromeda *arborea*,
　axillaris,
　calyculata,
　cassinaefolia,
　Catesbaei,
　fastigiata,

floribunda,
globulifera,
japonica,
Mariana ovalis,
ovalifolia,
pilifera,
polifolia,
recurva,
speciosa,
tetragona,
Angelica tree,
Aralia *japonica,*
  mandshurica,
  Sieboldii,
  spinosa,
Aralia. See Fatsia,
Arbutus Andrachne,
  Menziesii,
  Milleri,
  mucronata,
  photiniaefolia,
  procera,
  Rollisoni,
  serratifolia,
  Unedo,
  Unedo Croomei,
Arctostaphylos alpina,
  Uva-ursi,
Aristolochio Sipho,
Aronia Thorn,
Arrowwood,
Asimina triloba,

Aster albescens,
  cabulicus,
Atragene alpina,
Azalea *arborescens*,
  calendulacea,
  ledifolia,
  mollis,
  occidentalis,
  pontica,
  viscosa,
Azalea. See Rhododendron,
Azaleas, Ghent,
Azara microphylla,
  integrifolia,
  lanceolata,
  serrata,
Baccharis halimifolia,
  patagonica,
Band plant,
Bastard Acacia,
Bastard Box,
Baptisia nepalensis,
Beach or Sand Plum,
Bearberry,
Beef Suet tree,
Benthamia fragifera,
  japonica,
Benthamia. See Cornus,
Berberidopsis corallina,
Berberis Aquifolium,
  Aquifolium repens,
  aristata,

Bealei,
buxifolia,
congestiflora,
Darwinii,
dulcis,
empetrifolia,
Fortunei,
gracilis,
ilicifolia,
japonica,
Berberis ***microphylla***,
nepalensis,
nervosa,
pinnata,
sinensis,
stenophylla,
trifoliolata,
trifurca,
vulgaris,
Wallichiana,
Berchemia volubilis,
Bignonia capreolata,
grandiflora,
radicans,
Bignonia. See Tecoma,
Billardiera longiflora,
Billberry,
Birchberry,
Bird Cherry,
Bitter Sweet,
Bladder Senna,
Blue Apple berry,
Blueberry,

Bog Myrtle,
Bour tree,
Box, flowering,
Box Thorn,
Bow-wood,
Bridgesia spicata,
Bridgesia. See Ercilla,
Bryanthus erectus,
  empetriforrnis,
Buckeye, the,
Buckthorn, common,
Buddleia *crispa*,
  globosa,
  Lindleyana,
  paniculata,
Bupleurum fruticosum,
Butcher's Broom,
Caesalpinia *japonica*,
  sepiaria,
Calico bush,
Californian or Western Allspice,
Californian Fuchsia,
Calluna vulgaris,
Calophaca wolgarica,
Calycanthus floridus,
  occidentalis,
Canada Tea,
Caragana *Altagana*,
  arborescens,
  frutescens,
  microphylla,
  spinosa,
Cardiandra alternifolia,

Carolina Allspice,
Carpenteria californica,
Caryopteris Mastacanthus,
Casandra calyculata,
Cassinia fulvida,
Cassiope fastigiata,
  tetragona,
Castanea sativa,
  vesca,
  vulgaris,
Catalpa bignonioides,
  Bungei,
  Kaempferi,
  speciosa,
Cat Whim,
Ceanothus americanus,
  azureus,
  cuneatus,
  dentatus,
  pappilosus,
  rigidus,
  verrucosus,
Cedrela sinensis,
Celustrus scandens,
Celtis australis,
  occidentalis,
Cerasus *Caproniana multiplex*,
  Chamaecerasus,
  ilicifolius,
  Juliana,
  Launesiana,
  Laurocerasus,

   lusitanica,
   Mahaleb,
   Padus,
   Pseudocerasus,
   ranunculiflora,
   semperflorens,
   serrulata flore-pleno,
   Sieboldii,
   virginiana,
   vulgaris,
Cerasus. See Prunus,
Cercis canadensis,
  Siliquastrum,
Chaste tree,
Cherry, Bastard,
  common,
  ground,
  Laurel,
  St. Julian's,
Chimonanthus fragrans,
Chinese Akebia,
Chinese Pear tree,
  Quince,
Chionanthus retusa,
  virginica,
Choisya ternata,
Christ's Thorn,
Cistus crispus,
  formosus,
  ladaniferus,
  laevipes,
  laurifolius,

monspeliensis,
purpureus,
salvifolius,
Citharexylum cyanocarpum,
Citharexylum. See Rhapithamnus,
Citrus trifoliata,
Cladrastis amurensis,
tinctoria,
lutea,
Clammy Azalea,
Clammy Locust,
Clematis alpina,
austriaca,
azurea grandiflora,
cirrhosa,
caerulea,
Flammula,
florida,
Fortunei,
graveolens,
lanuginosa,
montana,
patens,
sibirica,
Viorna,
Vitalba,
Williamsii,
Clerodendron foetidum,
trichotomum,
Clethra acuminata,
alnifolia,
Climbing Berchemia,
Climbing Waxwork,

Cockspur Thorn,
Cocculus carolinus,
  laurifolius,
Colchican Bladder Nut,
Colletia *bictonensis*,
  cruciata,
  serratifolia,
  spinosa,
Colutea arborescens,
  cruenta,
  orientalis,
  sanguinea,
Comptonia asplenifolia,
Comptonia. See Myrica,
Constantinople Hazel,
Coral Barberry,
Coral Berry,
Corchorus japonicus,
Coriaria myrtifolia,
Cornel, the,
Cornelian Cherry,
Corokia Cotoneaster,
Coronilla Emerus,
Cernus alba,
  alternifolia,
  amomum,
  asperifolia,
  Baileyi,
  brachypoda,
  californica,
  canadensis,
  candidissima,
  capitata,

circinata,
florida,
Kousa,
macrophylla,
Mas,
Nuttalii,
officinalis,
paniculata,
pubescens,
sericea,
stolonifera,
tartarica,
sibirica,
Corylopsis Himalayana,
  pauciflora,
  spicata,
Corylus Avellana purpurea,
  Colurna,
Cotoneaster bacillaris,
  frigida,
  microphylla,
  Simonsii,
Cowberry,
Crataegus *arbutifolia*,
  Azarolus,
  Azarolus Aronia,
  Celsiana,
  coccinea,
  coccinea macrantha,
  cordata,
  Crus-galli,
  Douglasii,
  glabra,

nigra,
Oxyacantha,
parvifolia,
Pyracantha,
tanacetifolia,
Cucumber tree,
Currants, flowering,
Cydonia chinensis,
  japonica,
Cytisus *Adami*,
  albus,
  albus incarnatus,
  alpinus,
  biflorus,
  decumbens,
Cytisus *elongatus*,
  incarnatus,
  Laburnum,
  nigricans,
  purpureus,
  scoparius,
Daboecia polifolia,
Danae Laurus,
  racemosa,
Daphne alpina,
  altaica,
  Blagayana,
  Championi,
  Cneorum,
  collina,
  Fioniana,
  Fortunei,

Genkwa,
Laureola,
Mezereum,
petraea,
pontica,
rupestris,
sericea,
Daphniphyllum glaucescens,
Date Plum, the,
Desfontainea spinosa,
Desmodium penduliftorum,
Desmodium. See Lespedeza,
Deutzia crenata,
  Fortunei,
  gracilis,
  scabra,
Diervilla ***amabilis***,
  floribunda,
  grandiflora,
  multiflora,
  rosea,
Dimorphanthus mandshuricus,
Dimorphanthus. See Aralia,
Diospyros Kaki costata,
  lotus,
  virginiana,
Diplopappus chrysophyllus,
Diplopappus. See Cassinia,
Dirca palustris,
Discaria longispina,
  serratifolia,
Dockmackie,

Dogwood,
Drimys aromatica,
  Winteri,
Dutchman's Pipe,
Elaeagnus argentea,
  crispa,
  edulis,
  glabra,
  longipes,
  macrophylla,
  reflexus,
  rotundifolia,
Elder, Californian,
  Scarlet berried,
Embothrium coccineum,
Ephedra *monastachya*,
  vulgaris,
Epigaea repens,
Ercilla spicata,
Erica carnea,
  ciliaris,
  cineria,
  erecta,
  mediterranea,
  scoparia,
  Tetralix,
  vagans,
    vulgaris,
Eriobotrya japonica,
Eriobotrya. See Photinia,
Etna Broom,
Eucryphia pinnatifolia,
Eugenia apiculata,

Luma,
Ugni,
Euonymus americana,
  europaeus,
  fimbriatus,
  latifolius,
Eurybia Gunniana,
Evergreen Laburnum,
Escallonia floribunda,
  illinita,
  macrantha,
  montevidensis,
  Phillipiana,
  pterocladon,
  rubra,
Exochorda grandiflora,
Fabiana imbricata,
False Acacia,
Fatsia japonica,
Fendlera rupicola,
Fiery Thorn,
Fire Bush,
Flacourtia japonica,
Florida Dogwood,
Forsythia *Fortunei*,
  Sieboldii,
  suspensa,
  viridissima,
Fothergilla alnifolia,
Fraxinus *argentea*,
  Ornus,
  Ornus serotina alba,
  Ornus serotina violacea,

   Mariesii,
Fremontia californica,
Fuchsia *globosa*,
  macrostemma globosa,
  Riccartoni,
Garland Flower,
Garrya elliptica,
Gaultheria *nummulariae*,
  nummularioides,
  procumbens,
  repens,
  Shallon,
Genista aetnensis,
  anxantica,
  capitata,
  cinerea,
  daurica,
  elatior,
  ephedroides,
  germanica,
  hispanica,
  lusitanica,
  monosperma,
  pilosa,
  prostrata,
  radiata,
  ramosissima,
  sagittalis,
  tinctoria,
  tinctoria elatior,
  triangularis,
  triquetra,
Gleditschia triacanthos,

triacanthos pendula,
  sinensis,
  horrida,
Glycine chinensis,
  frutescens,
  sinensis,
Gordonia Lasianthus,
  pubescens,
Grabowskia boerhaaviaefolia,
Griselinia littoralis,
Ground Cistus,
Ground Laurel,
Groundsel Tree,
Guelder Rose,
Gum Cistus,
Gymnocladus canadensis,
  chinensis,
Hagberry,
Halesia diptera,
  hispida,
  parviflora,
  reticulata,
  tetraptera,
Halimodendron argenteum,
Hamamelis japonica,
  japonica arborea,
  japonica Zuccariniana,
  virginica,
Hare's Ear,
Hawthorn, the,
Hazel, the,
Heather, the Common,
Hedysarum multijugum,

Heimia salicifolia,
Heimia. See Nesaea,
Helianthemum *formosum*,
  halimifolium,
  laevipes,
  lasianthum,
  lavendulaefolium,
  libanotis,
  pilosum,
  polifolium,
  pulverulentum,
  serpyllifolium,
  umbellatum,
  vulgare,
  vulgare nummularium,
  vulgare barbatum,
  vulgare mutabile,
  vulgare grandiflorum,
  vulgare ovalifolium,
  vulgare hysopifolium,
Hemp Tree,
Hippophae rhamnoides,
Holboellia latifolia,
Holly, the,
Honey Locust,
Honeysuckles,
Hop tree,
Hornbeam,
Horse Chestnut,
Hortensia opuloides,
Humming Bird's Trumpet,
Hybiscus syriacus,
  syriacus vars.,

Hydrangea arborescens,
  hortensis,
  hortensis vars.,
  quercifolia,
  scandens,
  paniculata,
  paniculata grandiflora,
Hydrangea, climbing,
Hymenanthera crassifolia,
Hypericum Androsaemum,
  aureum,
  calycinum,
  elatum,
  hircinum,
  Moserianum,
  oblongifolium,
  Hookerianum,
  nepalensis,
  prolificum,
  uralum,
Idesia polycarpa,
Ilex Aquifolium,
  Aquifolium vars.,
  opaca,
Illicium anisatum,
  floridanum,
  religiosum,
Indian Azalea,
Indigofera Dosua,
  floribunda,
  Gerardiana,
Itea virginica,
Jamesia americana,

Japanese Storax,
Japan Medlar, or Quince,
Jasminum fruticans,
  humile,
  nudiflorum,
  officinale,
  pubigerum glabrum,
  revolutum,
  Wallichianum,
Jerusalem Sage,
Job's Tears,
Judas tree,
June Berry, the,
Kadsura japonica,
Kalmia angustifolia,
  glauca,
  hirsuta,
  latifolia,
  latifolia vars.,
Kentucky Coffee Tree,
Kerria japonica,
Koelreuteria paniculata,
Labrador Tea,
Laburnum Adami,
  alpinum,
  caramanicum,
  vulgare,
Lady's Bower,
Lapageria rosea,
Lardizabala biternata,
Laurel, Alexandrian,
  American Great,
  Cherry,

Ground,
Mountain,
Portugal,
Sheep,
Spurge,
Laurustinus,
Lavender, common,
Lavandula *Spica*,
  vera,
Lavatera arborea,
Leather Wood,
Ledum *buxifolium*,
  groenlandicum,
  latifolium,
  palustre,
Leiophyllum buxifolium,
  thymifolia,
Lemon Scented Verbena,
Lespedeza bicolor,
Leucothoe axillaris,
  Catesbaei,
  Davisiae,
  floribunda,
  recurva,
Leycesteria formosa,
Ligustrina amurensis,
Ligustrum *amurense*,
  californicum,
  glabrum,
  Ibota,
  Ibota villosum,
  japonicum,

Ligustrum *Kellermanni*
  lucidum,
  magnoliaefolium,
  ovalifolium,
  Sieboldii,
  sinense,
  strictum,
  villosum,
  vulgare,
Lily, the Mound,
Limonia Laureola,
Linden Tree,
Ling, the common,
Linnaea borealis,
Lippia citriodora,
Liriodendron tulipifera,
Loblolly Bay,
Locust, common,
Lonicera *brachypoda*,
  Caprifolium,
  flexuosa,
  fragrantissima,
  Periclymenum,
  sempervirens,
  Standishii,
  tatarica,
  Xylosteum,
Loquat, the,
Loropetalum chinense,
Lycium barbarum,
  europaeum,
Lyonia *ligustrina*,
  paniculata,

Maclura aurantiaca,
Mahaleb, or Perfumed Cherry,
Mahonia Aquifolium,
  Bealei,
  facicularis,
  Fortunei,
  glumacea,
  gracilis,
  Hookeri,
  japonica,
  nepalensis,
  Neumanii,
  repens,
  trifoliolata,
  trifurca,
Magnolia acuminata,
  auriculata,
  Campbelii,
  conspicua,
  conspicua Alexandrina,
  conspicua Soulangeana,
  conspicua Soulangeana nigra,
  conspicua Soulangeana Norbertii,
  conspicua Soulangeana speciosa,
  cordata,
  Fraseri,
  glauca,
  grandiflora,
  Halleana,
  Lennei,
  macrophylla,
  obovata discolor,

parviflora,
purpurea,
stellata,
tripetala,
Umbrella,
Yulan,
Malachodendron ovatum,
Mallow, Syrian,
Mallow tree,
Malus microcarpa floribunda,
Manna Ash,
Marsh Ledum,
Mayflower, New England,
Medicago arborea,
Medlar, common,
Menispermum canadense,
Menziesia. See Daboecia; Phylodoce; and Lyonia,
Menziesia caerulea,
  empetrifolia,
  globularis,
  polifolia,
Mespilus arbutifolia,
  germanica,
  grandiflora,
  Smithii,
Mexican Orange Flower,
Mezereon, the,
Microglossa albescens,
Mitchella repens,
Mitraria coccinea,
Mitre pod, scarlet,

Mock Orange,
Monk's Pepper-tree,
Moonseed,
Mountain Ash,
Mountain Laurel,
Moutan Paeony,
Myrica asplenifolia,
  californica,
  cerifera,
  Gale,
Myricaria germanica,
Myrobalan Plum,
Myrtle, Bog,
  Common,
  Californian Wax,
  Common Candle-berry,
  Sand,
Myrtus communis,
  Luma,
  Ugni,
Neillia opulifolia,
  thyrsiflora,
Nepaul White Beam,
Nesaea salicifolia,
Neviusa alabamensis,
New Jersey Tea,
Nine Bark,
Nuttalia cerasiformis,
Old Man's beard,
Olearia *dentata*,
  Forsterii,
  Gunniana,
  Haastii,

macrodonta,
Ononis arvensis,
Orange Ball tree,
Ornus europea,
Osage Orange,
Osmanthus Aquifolium ilicifolius,
  Aquifolium illicifolius myrtifolius,
Osoberry,
Ostrya carpinifolia,
  virginica,
  vulgaris,
Oxydendrum arboreum,
Ozothamnus rosmarinifolius,
Paeonia Moutan,
Pagoda-tree, Chinese,
Paliurus aculeatus,
  australis,
Papaw, the Virginian,
Parrotia persica,
Partridge Berry,
Passiflora caerulea,
Paulownia imperialis,
Pavia californica,
  discolor,
  flava,
  humilis,
Pavia macrocarpa,
  macrostachya,
  rubra,
Pavia, See Aesculus,
Pepper-plant, Tasmanian,
Pepper-tree,

Periploca graeca,
Periwinkles,
Pernettya mucronata,
Persimmon, the,
Philadelphus coronarius,
  chinensis,
  floribundus,
  Gordonianus,
  grandiflorus,
  hirsutus,
  inodorus,
  latifolius,
  Lemoinei,
  Lewisii,
  mexicanus,
  microphyllus,
  satzumi,
  speciosus,
  triflorus,
Phillyrea angustifolia,
  decora,
  latifolia,
  laurifolia,
  ligustrifolia,
  media,
  neapolitana,
  obliqua,
  oleaefolia,
  rosmarinifolia,
  Vilmoriniana,
Phlomis fruticosa,
Photinia arbutifolia,

Benthumiana,
  japonica,
  serrulata,
Phyllodoce taxifolia,
  caerulea,
Pieris floribunda,
  japonica,
  Mariana,
  ovalifolia,
Pipe tree,
Piptanthus nepalensis,
Pittosporum Tobira,
  undulatum,
Plagianthus Lyalli,
  Lampeni,
  pulohellus,
Planera acuminata,
  crenata, 134
  Richardi,
Planera, See Zelkova,
Poison Elder,
Poison Ivy,
Poison Oak,
Poison Vine,
Polycarpa Maximowiczii,
Pomegranate,
Pontic Daphne,
Portugal Laurel,
Potato tree,
Potentilla fruticosa,
Prickly Ivy,
Privets,
Prunopsis Lindleyi,

Prunus Amygdalus,
  Amygdalus dulcis,
  Avium Juliana,
  Boissieri,
  cerasifera,
  cerasifera Pissardii,
  Cerasus,
Prunus Chamaecerasus,
  Davidiana,
  divaricata,
  domestica,
  ilicifolia,
  Launesiana,
  Laurocerasus,
  lusitanica,
  Mahaleb,
  maritima,
  Myrobalana,
  nana,
  Padus,
  paniculata flore-pleno,
  pennsylvanica,
  Persica flore-pleno,
  Pissardii,
  Pseudo-cerasus,
  Puddum,
  serotina,
  sinensis,
  spinosa,
  tomentosa,
  triloba,
  virginiana,
  virgata,

Ptelea trifoliata,
Pterpstyrax hispidum,
Punica Granatum,
Purple Broom,
Purple Hazel,
Pyrus amygdaliformis.,
  Aria,
  Aucuparia,
  americana,
  angustifolia,
  baccata,
  Bollwylleriana,
  coronaria,
  domestica,
  floribunda,
  germanica,
  japonica,
  prunifolia,
  Malus floribunda,
  rivularis,
  salvaefolia,
  salicifolia,
  sinensis of Lindley,
  sinensis,
  sinica,
  Smithii,
  torminalis,
  vestita,
Quince, Japanese,
  Chinese,
Rabbit berry,
Red Osier Dogwood,
Restharrow,

Rhamnus Alaternus,
  alpinus,
  catharticus,
  Frangula,
Rhaphiolepis japonica integerrima,
  ovata
Rhaphithamnus cyanocarpus,
Rhododendron ***aeruginosum***,
  arborescens,
  arboreum,
  argenteum,
  Aucklandii,
  barbatum,
  calendulaceum,
  californicum,
  campanulatum,
  Campbelli,
  campylocarpum,
  catawbiense,
Rhododendron ***Chamaecistus***,
  chrysanthum,
  ciliatum,
  cinnabarinum,
  Collettianum,
  dahuricum,
  eximium,
  Falconeri,
  ferrugineum,
  flavuni,
  Fortunei,
  glaucum,
  hirsutum,
  Hodgsoni,

indicum,
lanatum,
ledifolium,
maximum,
molle,
niveum,
occidentale,
parvifolium,
ponticum,
ponticum azaleoides,
ponticum deciduum,
racemosum,
Rhodora,
Roylei,
Smirnowii,
Thompsoni,
Ungernii,
viscosum,
Wallichii,
Wilsoni,
Rhododendrons, hardy hybrid,
Rhodora canadensis,
Rhodothamnus Chamaecistus,
Rhodotypos Kerrioides,
Rhus caroliniana,
  coccinea,
  Cotinus,
  elegans,
  glabra,
  sanguinea,
  succedanea,
  Toxicodendron,
  typhina,

venenata,
vernix,
Ribes alpinum pumilum aureum,
  aureum,
  Beatonii,
  cereum,
  floridum,
  Gordonianum,
  inebrians,
  Loudonii,
  missouriense,
  multiflorum,
  pennsylvanicum,
  sanguineum,
  speciosum,
Robinia ambigua,
  dubia,
  echinata,
  glutinosa,
  Halimodendron,
  hispida,
  Pseud-Acacia,
  viscosa,
Rock Abelia,
Rock Daphne,
Rock Rose, the,
Rosa alba,
  arvensis,
  bengalensis,
  bracteata,
  canina,
Rosa centifolia,

damascena,
diversifolia,
Eglanteria,
ferox,
gallica,
hemisphaerica,
indica,
indica minima,
indica semperflorens,
Lawrenceana,
lutea,
minima,
pimpinellifolia,
repens,
rugosa,
sempervirens,
semperflorens minima,
spinosissima,
sulphurea,
villosa,
Rose Acacia,
Rose Bay,
Rose of Sharon,
Rosmarinus officinalis,
Rosemary, common,
Rosemary, wild,
Rowan-tree,
Rubus arcticus,
  australis,
  biflorus,
  deliciosus,
  fruticosus,
  laciniatus,

nutkanus,
   odoratus,
   rosaefolius,
   spectabilis,
Ruscus aculeatus,
   Hypophyllum,
   racemosus,
St. Anthony's Nut,
St. Dabeoc's Heath,
St. Peter's Wort,
Sand Myrtle,
Sallow thorn,
Salt tree,
Sambucus californica,
   glauca,
   nigra,
   racemosa,
   rosaeflora,
Schizandra chinensis,
   coccinea,
Schizophragma hydrangeoides,
Scorpion Senna,
Sea Buckthorn,
Sea Purslane,
Service tree, true,
Sheepberry,
Sheep Laurel,
Shepherdia argentea,
   canadensis,
Shrubs for seaside planting,
   for town planting,
Siberian Crab,
Siberian Pea tree,

Sida pulchella,
Silk grass,
Silver Berry,
Skimmia Fortunei,
  japonica,
  Laureola,
  oblata,
  rubella,
Smilax aspera,
Smoke Plant,
Snowberry,
Snowdrop Tree,
Soap Tree,
Solanum crispum,
  Dulcamara,
Sophora japonica,
  tetraptera,
Sorbus Americana,
  domestica,
Sorrel-tree,
Spanish Broom; White,
Spanish Chestnut, Sweet,
Spartium junceum,
  acutifolium,
  aetnensis,
  radiatum,
Spindle tree,
Spiraea altaica,
  altaicensis,
  ariaefolia,
  bella,
  Blumei,
  bullata,

callosa,
cana,
cantoniensis,
ceanothifolia,
chamaedrifolia,
confusa,
crispifolia,
decumbens,
discolor ariaefolia,
Douglasii,
fissa,
flagellata,
Fortunei,
grandiflora,
hypericifolia,
japonica,
laevigata,
Lindleyana,
media,
nana,
oblongifolia,
opulifolia,
prunifolia,
Reevesiana,
rotundifolia,
salicifolia,
sorbifolia,
Thunbergii,
tomentosa,
triloba,
trilobata,
umbrosa,
Spurge Laurel,

Stag's Horn Sumach,
Staphylea colchica,
  pinnata,
  trifolia,
Stauntonia haxaphylla,
  latifolia,
Strawberry Tree,
Stuartia grandiflora,
  marylandica,
  pentagyna,
  pseudo-Camellia,
  virginica,
Styphnolobium japonicum,
Styrax americana,
  japonica,
  officinalis,
  pulverulenta,
  serrulata virgata,
Sumach,
Swamp Dogwood,
Swamp Honeysuckle,
Sweet Amber,
Sweet Fern,
Sweet Gale,
Sweet Viburnum,
Symphoria racemosus,
Symphoricarpus occidentalis,
  racemosus,
  vulgaris,
Syrian Mallow,
Syringa chinensis,
  dubia,
  rothomagensis,

Emodi,
japonica,
amurensis,
Josikaea,
persica,
vulgaris,
Symplocos japonica,
tinctoria,
Tamarix gallica,
africana,
parviflora,
tetrandra,
Tam Furze,
Tansy-leaved Thorn,
Tasmania aromatica,
Tea, Labrador,
Tea tree,
Tecoma grandiflora,
radicans,
Thyrsanthus frutescens,
Tilia ***europea***,
intermedia,
vulgaris,
Tree Mallow,
Tree of Heaven,
Trees for seaside planting,
for town planting,
Trumpet Flower,
Tulip tree,
Tutsan, the,
Ulex europaeus,
nanus,
Vaccinium corymbosum,

 Myrtillus,
 pennsylvanicum,
 Vitis-Idea,
Veronica pinquifolia,
 Travereii,
Vinca major,
 minor,
Vinegar tree,
Venetian Sumach,
Verbena, Lemon-scented,
Verbena triphylla,
Viburnum acerifolium,
 Awafukii,
Viburnum daburicum,
 dentatum,
 Fortunei,
 laevigatum,
 Lantana,
 Lentago,
 macrocephalum,
 nudum,
 Opulus,
 pauciflorum,
 plicatum,
 prunifolium,
 pyrifolium,
 reticulatum,
 Tinus,
Virgilia lutea,
Virgilia. See Cladrastis,
Virgin's Bower,
Vitex Agnas-castus,
Vitis heterophylla humulifolia,

Wayfaring tree,
Weigelia. See Diervilla,
Weigelia amabilis,
  floribunda,
  rosea,
White Bean tree,
White Kerria,
Whortlebury,
Wig tree,
Wild Rosemary,
Wintera aromatica,
Winter Flower,
Winter's Bark,
Wistaria chinensis,
  frutescens,
  japonica,
  multijuga,
  sinensis,
Witch Hazel, the,
Wolf Berry,
Woody Nightshade,
Xanthoceras sorbifolia,
Xanthoriza apiifolia,
Xylosteum dumetorum,
Yellow root,
Yellow wood,
Yucca filamentosa,
  gloriosa,
Yulan, the,
Zauschneria californica,
Zenobia speciosa,
Zelkova acuminata,
  crenata,

cretica,
japonica.

www.bookjungle.com *email:* sales@bookjungle.com *fax:* 630-214-0564 *mail:* Book Jungle PO Box 2226 Champaign, IL 61825

The Codes Of Hammurabi And Moses
W. W. Davies

QTY

The discovery of the Hammurabi Code is one of the greatest achievements of archaeology, and is of paramount interest, not only to the student of the Bible, but also to all those interested in ancient history...

Religion   **ISBN:** *1-59462-338-4*   Pages:132
                                              MSRP $12.95

The Theory of Moral Sentiments
Adam Smith

QTY

This work from 1749. contains original theories of conscience amd moral judgment and it is the foundation for systemof morals.

Philosophy   **ISBN:** *1-59462-777-0*   Pages:536
                                              MSRP $19.95

Jessica's First Prayer
Hesba Stretton

QTY

In a screened and secluded corner of one of the many railway-bridges which span the streets of London there could be seen a few years ago, from five o'clock every morning until half past eight, a tidily set-out coffee-stall, consisting of a trestle and board, upon which stood two large tin cans, with a small fire of charcoal burning under each so as to keep the coffee boiling during the early hours of the morning when the work-people were thronging into the city on their way to their daily toil...

                                              Pages:84
Childrens   **ISBN:** *1-59462-373-2*   *MSRP $9.95*

My Life and Work
Henry Ford

QTY

Henry Ford revolutionized the world with his implementation of mass production for the Model T automobile. Gain valuable business insight into his life and work with his own auto-biography... "We have only started on our development of our country we have not as yet, with all our talk of wonderful progress, done more than scratch the surface. The progress has been wonderful enough but..."

                                              Pages:300
Biographies/ **ISBN:** *1-59462-198-5*   *MSRP $21.95*

www.bookjungle.com email: sales@bookjungle.com fax: 630-214-0564 mail: Book Jungle PO Box 2226 Champaign, IL 61825

The Art of Cross-Examination
Francis Wellman

QTY

I presume it is the experience of every author, after his first book is published upon an important subject, to be almost overwhelmed with a wealth of ideas and illustrations which could readily have been included in his book, and which to his own mind, at least, seem to make a second edition inevitable. Such certainly was the case with me; and when the first edition had reached its sixth impression in five months, I rejoiced to learn that it seemed to my publishers that the book had met with a sufficiently favorable reception to justify a second and considerably enlarged edition. ..

Reference   ISBN: *1-59462-647-2*   Pages:412   MSRP *$19.95*

On the Duty of Civil Disobedience
Henry David Thoreau

QTY

Thoreau wrote his famous essay, On the Duty of Civil Disobedience, as a protest against an unjust but popular war and the immoral but popular institution of slave-owning. He did more than write—he declined to pay his taxes, and was hauled off to gaol in consequence. Who can say how much this refusal of his hastened the end of the war and of slavery ?

Law   ISBN: *1-59462-747-9*   Pages:48   MSRP *$7.45*

Dream Psychology Psychoanalysis for Beginners
Sigmund Freud

QTY

Sigmund Freud, born Sigismund Schlomo Freud (May 6, 1856 - September 23, 1939), was a Jewish-Austrian neurologist and psychiatrist who co-founded the psychoanalytic school of psychology. Freud is best known for his theories of the unconscious mind, especially involving the mechanism of repression; his redefinition of sexual desire as mobile and directed towards a wide variety of objects; and his therapeutic techniques, especially his understanding of transference in the therapeutic relationship and the presumed value of dreams as sources of insight into unconscious desires.

Psychology   ISBN: *1-59462-905-6*   Pages:196   MSRP *$15.45*

The Miracle of Right Thought
Orison Swett Marden

QTY

Believe with all of your heart that you will do what you were made to do. When the mind has once formed the habit of holding cheerful, happy, prosperous pictures, it will not be easy to form the opposite habit. It does not matter how improbable or how far away this realization may see, or how dark the prospects may be, if we visualize them as best we can, as vividly as possible, hold tenaciously to them and vigorously struggle to attain them, they will gradually become actualized, realized in the life. But a desire, a longing without endeavor, a yearning abandoned or held indifferently will vanish without realization.

Self Help   ISBN: *1-59462-644-8*   Pages:360   MSRP *$25.45*

www.bookjungle.com email: sales@bookjungle.com fax: 630-214-0564 mail: Book Jungle PO Box 2226 Champaign, IL 61825

QTY

- [ ] **The Rosicrucian Cosmo-Conception Mystic Christianity** by *Max Heindel* ISBN: *1-59462-188-8* **$38.95**
  The Rosicrucian Cosmo-conception is not dogmatic, neither does it appeal to any other authority than the reason of the student. It is: not controversial, but is: sent forth in the, hope that it may help to clear... New Age/Religion Pages 646

- [ ] **Abandonment To Divine Providence** by *Jean-Pierre de Caussade* ISBN: *1-59462-228-0* **$25.95**
  "The Rev. Jean Pierre de Caussade was one of the most remarkable spiritual writers of the Society of Jesus in France in the 18th Century. His death took place at Toulouse in 1751. His works have gone through many editions and have been republished... Inspirational/Religion Pages 400

- [ ] **Mental Chemistry** by *Charles Haanel* ISBN: *1-59462-192-6* **$23.95**
  Mental Chemistry allows the change of material conditions by combining and appropriately utilizing the power of the mind. Much like applied chemistry creates something new and unique out of careful combinations of chemicals the mastery of mental chemistry... New Age Pages 354

- [ ] **The Letters of Robert Browning and Elizabeth Barret Barrett 1845-1846 vol II** ISBN: *1-59462-193-4* **$35.95**
  by *Robert Browning* and *Elizabeth Barrett*
  Biographies Pages 596

- [ ] **Gleanings In Genesis (volume I)** by *Arthur W. Pink* ISBN: *1-59462-130-6* **$27.45**
  Appropriately has Genesis been termed "the seed plot of the Bible" for in it we have, in germ form, almost all of the great doctrines which are afterwards fully developed in the books of Scripture which follow... Religion/Inspirational Pages 420

- [ ] **The Master Key** by *L. W. de Laurence* ISBN: *1-59462-001-6* **$30.95**
  In no branch of human knowledge has there been a more lively increase of the spirit of research during the past few years than in the study of Psychology, Concentration and Mental Discipline. The requests for authentic lessons in Thought Control, Mental Discipline and... New Age/Business Pages 422

- [ ] **The Lesser Key Of Solomon Goetia** by *L. W. de Laurence* ISBN: *1-59462-092-X* **$9.95**
  This translation of the first book of the "Lerngton" which is now for the first time made accessible to students of Talismanic Magic was done, after careful collation and edition, from numerous Ancient Manuscripts in Hebrew, Latin, and French... New Age/Occult Pages 92

- [ ] **Rubaiyat Of Omar Khayyam** by *Edward Fitzgerald* ISBN: *1-59462-332-5* **$13.95**
  Edward Fitzgerald, whom the world has already learned, in spite of his own efforts to remain within the shadow of anonymity, to look upon as one of the rarest poets of the century, was born at Bredfield, in Suffolk, on the 31st of March, 1809. He was the third son of John Purcell... Music Pages 172

- [ ] **Ancient Law** by *Henry Maine* ISBN: *1-59462-128-4* **$29.95**
  The chief object of the following pages is to indicate some of the earliest ideas of mankind, as they are reflected in Ancient Law, and to point out the relation of those ideas to modern thought. Religion/History Pages 452

- [ ] **Far-Away Stories** by *William J. Locke* ISBN: *1-59462-129-2* **$19.45**
  "Good wine needs no bush, but a collection of mixed vintages does. And this book is just such a collection. Some of the stories I do not want to remain buried for ever in the museum files of dead magazine-numbers an author's not unpardonable vanity..." Fiction Pages 272

- [ ] **Life of David Crockett** by *David Crockett* ISBN: *1-59462-250-7* **$27.45**
  "Colonel David Crockett was one of the most remarkable men of the times in which he lived. Born in humble life, but gifted with a strong will, an indomitable courage, and unremitting perseverance... Biographies/New Age Pages 424

- [ ] **Lip-Reading** by *Edward Nitchie* ISBN: *1-59462-206-X* **$25.95**
  Edward B. Nitchie, founder of the New York School for the Hard of Hearing, now the Nitchie School of Lip-Reading, Inc, wrote "LIP-READING Principles and Practice". The development and perfecting of this meritorious work on lip-reading was an undertaking... How-to Pages 400

- [ ] **A Handbook of Suggestive Therapeutics, Applied Hypnotism, Psychic Science** ISBN: *1-59462-214-0* **$24.95**
  by *Henry Munro*
  Health/New Age/Health/Self-help Pages 376

- [ ] **A Doll's House: and Two Other Plays** by *Henrik Ibsen* ISBN: *1-59462-112-8* **$19.95**
  Henrik Ibsen created this classic when in revolutionary 1848 Rome. Introducing some striking concepts in playwriting for the realist genre, this play has been studied the world over. Fiction/Classics/Plays 308

- [ ] **The Light of Asia** by *sir Edwin Arnold* ISBN: *1-59462-204-3* **$13.95**
  In this poetic masterpiece, Edwin Arnold describes the life and teachings of Buddha. The man who was to become known as Buddha to the world was born as Prince Gautama of India but he rejected the worldly riches and abandoned the reigns of power when... Religion/History/Biographies Pages 170

- [ ] **The Complete Works of Guy de Maupassant** by *Guy de Maupassant* ISBN: *1-59462-157-8* **$16.95**
  "For days and days, nights and nights, I had dreamed of that first kiss which was to consecrate our engagement, and I knew not on what spot I should put my lips..." Fiction/Classics Pages 240

- [ ] **The Art of Cross-Examination** by *Francis L. Wellman* ISBN: *1-59462-309-0* **$26.95**
  Written by a renowned trial lawyer, Wellman imparts his experience and uses case studies to explain how to use psychology to extract desired information through questioning. How-to/Science/Reference Pages 408

- [ ] **Answered or Unanswered?** by *Louisa Vaughan* ISBN: *1-59462-248-5* **$10.95**
  Miracles of Faith in China
  Religion Pages 112

- [ ] **The Edinburgh Lectures on Mental Science (1909)** by *Thomas* ISBN: *1-59462-008-3* **$11.95**
  This book contains the substance of a course of lectures recently given by the writer in the Queen Street Hall, Edinburgh. Its purpose is to indicate the Natural Principles governing the relation between Mental Action and Material Conditions... New Age/Psychology Pages 148

- [ ] **Ayesha** by *H. Rider Haggard* ISBN: *1-59462-301-5* **$24.95**
  Verily and indeed it is the unexpected that happens! Probably if there was one person upon the earth from whom the Editor of this, and of a certain previous history, did not expect to hear again... Classics Pages 380

- [ ] **Ayala's Angel** by *Anthony Trollope* ISBN: *1-59462-352-X* **$29.95**
  The two girls were both pretty, but Lucy who was twenty-one who supposed to be simple and comparatively unattractive, whereas Ayala was credited, as her Bombwhat romantic name might show, with poetic charm and a taste for romance. Ayala when her father died was nineteen... Fiction Pages 484

- [ ] **The American Commonwealth** by *James Bryce* ISBN: *1-59462-286-8* **$34.45**
  An interpretation of American democratic political theory. It examines political mechanics and society from the perspective of Scotsman James Bryce
  Politics Pages 572

- [ ] **Stories of the Pilgrims** by *Margaret P. Pumphrey* ISBN: *1-59462-116-0* **$17.95**
  This book explores pilgrims religious oppression in England as well as their escape to Holland and eventual crossing to America on the Mayflower, and their early days in New England... History Pages 268

www.bookjungle.com email: sales@bookjungle.com fax: 630-214-0564 mail: Book Jungle PO Box 2226 Champaign, IL 61825

QTY

The Fasting Cure *by Sinclair Upton* ISBN: *1-59462-222-1* **$13.95**
In the Cosmopolitan Magazine for May, 1910, and in the Contemporary Review (London) for April, 1910, I published an article dealing with my experiences in fasting. I have written a great many magazine articles, but never one which attracted so much attention... *New Age/Self Help/Health Pages 164*

Hebrew Astrology *by Sepharial* ISBN: *1-59462-308-2* **$13.45**
In these days of advanced thinking it is a matter of common observation that we have left many of the old landmarks behind and that we are now pressing forward to greater heights and to a wider horizon than that which represented the mind-content of our progenitors... *Astrology Pages 144*

Thought Vibration or The Law of Attraction in the Thought World ISBN: *1-59462-127-6* **$12.95**
by William Walker Atkinson *Psychology/Religion Pages 144*

Optimism *by Helen Keller* ISBN: *1-59462-108-X* **$15.95**
Helen Keller was blind, deaf, and mute since 19 months old, yet famously learned how to overcome these handicaps, communicate with the world, and spread her lectures promoting optimism. An inspiring read for everyone... *Biographies/Inspirational Pages 84*

Sara Crewe *by Frances Burnett* ISBN: *1-59462-360-0* **$9.45**
In the first place, Miss Minchin lived in London. Her home was a large, dull, tall one, in a large, dull square, where all the houses were alike, and all the sparrows were alike, and where all the door-knockers made the same heavy sound... *Childrens/Classic Pages 88*

The Autobiography of Benjamin Franklin *by Benjamin Franklin* ISBN: *1-59462-135-7* **$24.95**
The Autobiography of Benjamin Franklin has probably been more extensively read than any other American historical work, and no other book of its kind has had such ups and downs of fortune. Franklin lived for many years in England, where he was agent... *Biographies/History Pages 332*

Name	
Email	
Telephone	
Address	
City, State ZIP	

☐ Credit Card   ☐ Check / Money Order

Credit Card Number	
Expiration Date	
Signature	

Please Mail to: Book Jungle
                    PO Box 2226
                    Champaign, IL 61825
or Fax to: 630-214-0564

ORDERING INFORMATION

web: *www.bookjungle.com*
email: *sales@bookjungle.com*
fax: *630-214-0564*
mail: *Book Jungle PO Box 2226 Champaign, IL 61825*
or PayPal *to sales@bookjungle.com*

Please contact us for bulk discounts

DIRECT-ORDER TERMS

20% Discount if You Order Two or More Books
Free Domestic Shipping!
Accepted: Master Card, Visa, Discover, American Express

www.ingramcontent.com/pod-product-compliance
Lightning Source LLC
Chambersburg PA
CBHW080241170426
43192CB00014BA/2516